Jerry
1717
Denison, TX. 75020
214-519-4210

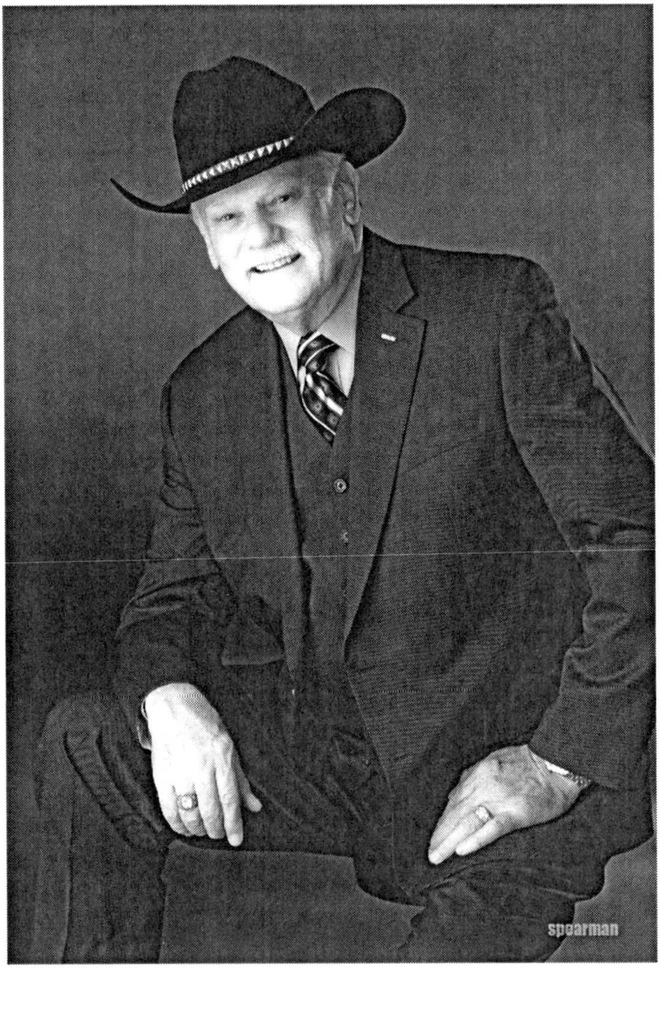
spearman

12 Ways to Walk with God

A Serious Study of Christian Doctrines in a Friendly, Fun-Reading Format

Dr. Buddy Merrick

CROSSBOOKS

CrossBooks™
A Division of LifeWay
1663 Liberty Drive
Bloomington, IN 47403
www.crossbooks.com
Phone: 1-866-879-0502

© 2013 Dr. M. S. Buddy Merrick. All rights reserved.

No part of this book may be reproduced, stored in a retrieval system, or transmitted by any means without the written permission of the author.

First published by CrossBooks 4/15/2013

ISBN: 978-1-4627-2676-9 (sc)
ISBN: 978-1-4627-2675-2 (hc)
ISBN: 978-1-4627-2677-6 (e)

Library of Congress Control Number: 2013906489

Printed in the United States of America.

This book is printed on acid-free paper.

Because of the dynamic nature of the Internet, any web addresses or links contained in this book may have changed since publication and may no longer be valid. The views expressed in this work are solely those of the author and do not necessarily reflect the views of the publisher, and the publisher hereby disclaims any responsibility for them.

ABOUT THE COVER:

"Jesus Our Shepherd" is a spectacular bronze sculpture created by Beverly Paddleford of Lander, Wyoming.

Walking alongside the Savior was the bellwether sheep, a ram who truly loved the shepherd and never left his side. Knowing that, the shepherd hung a bell around his neck, and when lost sheep heard the bell, they'd follow the sound and find their way home, knowing the bellwether would be near the Shepherd.

"Oh Lord, let us walk like Bellwether Sheep, always loving, always trusting, always near You, that others could follow, too, as we Walk With God, in the knowledge of His Word and the loving presence of Jesus our Shepherd. And, when others are lost, may the sound of our testimony lead them into Your Presence."

That's what this book is all about.

"Study to shew thyself approved unto God,
a workman that needeth not to be ashamed,
rightly dividing the word of truth"
(II Timothy 2:15)

Table of Contents

Foreword   ...Page xi

Prologue   ...Page xiii

I. Walk with the Word
Bibliology - The Bible, the Word of God
Preface   ...Page 1
The Sixty-six Books   ...Page 3
Divine Origin of the Bible   ...Page 6
Inspiration of the Bible   ...Page 7
The Bible Is Affirmed by Christ   ...Page 8
The Bible Is Affirmed by Paul   ...Page 9
The Bible Is Affirmed by Peter   ...Page 9
Inerrancy of the Bible   ...Page 9
Internal and External Evidences   ...Page 11
Canonicity of the Bible   ...Page 14
Summary   ...Page 16

II. Walk in the World
Anthropology - Why are we here anyway?
Preface   ...Page 19
Origin of Man   ...Page 20
The Material Part of Man   ...Page 22
The Nonmaterial Part of Man   ...Page 23
The Origin of the Soul   ...Page 24
Fall of Man   ...Page 24
Summary   ...Page 25

III. Walk Away from Sin
Hamartiology - Sin and What it Does to Us
Preface   ...Page 29

Original Sin   ...Page 32
The Punishment for Sin   ...Page 34
We Are Saved from Sin   ...Page 35
Summary   ...Page 37

IV. Walk Saved
Soteriology - All about Salvation, so Rich and Free

Preface   ...Page 39
The Atonement   ...Page 40
Limited Atonement   ...Page 44
Unlimited Atonement   ...Page 44
The Process of Salvation: the Work of the Father   ...Page 45
The Process of Salvation: the Work of the Son   ...Page 46
The Process of Salvation: the Work of the Spirit   ...Page 48
The Process of Salvation: the Work of the Believer   ...Page 49
Grace   ...Page 51
Regeneration   ...Page 53
Once Saved, Always Saved   ...Page 55
Summary   ...Page 56

V. Walk with Jesus
Christology - Is He was, or is He is?

Preface   ...Page 61
Jesus Is... Prophesy in the Old Testament,
Fulfilment in the New   ...Page 65
Prophesied and Fulfilled: The Life of Jesus   ...Page 67
Prophesied and Fulfilled: The Death of Jesus   ...Page 69
Prophesied and Fulfilled: The Victory of Jesus   ...Page 70
The Humanity of Christ   ...Page 71
The Deity of Christ   ...Page 71
The Hypostatic Union of Christ   ...Page 73
Jesus' Present Work   ...Page 74
Jesus' Future Work   ...Page 76
The Forever Reign of Jesus   ...Page 77

VI. Walk with the Holy Spirit
Pneumatology - Is the Holy Spirit a thing or is it a Him?
Preface   ...Page 79
The Personhood of the Holy Spirit   ...Page 80
The Deity of the Holy Spirit   ...Page 81
The Work of the Holy Spirit   ...Page 82
Oil, Water and Wind   ...Page 83
The Holy Spirit in Revelation and Inspiration   ...Page 84
The Ministry of the Holy Spirit in the Old Testament   ...Page 84
The Ministry of the Holy Spirit in the New Testament   ...Page 85
The Baptism of the Holy Spirit   ...Page 86
The Gifts of the Spirit   ...Page 88
Summary   ...Page 94

VII. Walk with God
Theology Proper - Is God really real?
Preface   ...Page 97
The Existence of God   ...Page 98
The Atheist   ...Page 99
God's Revelation   ...Page 100
The Attributes of God   ...Page 101
The Decrees of God   ...Page 103
Summary   ...Page 103

VIII. Walk with the Triune God
Trinitarianism - The Trinity: Father, Son and Holy Ghost
Preface   ...Page 107
The Bible Tells of the Triune God   ...Page 108
"Trinity" in the Bible   ...Page 110
The Work of God and Jesus Compared   ...Page 111
The Work of God the Holy Spirit and Jesus Compared   ...Page 111
Summary   ...Page 112

IX. Walk with Angels
Angelology - Angels all around us - Devils, too
Preface   ...Page 117

Angels and Us   ...Page 119
Demons   ...Page 120
How Do We Know That Angels Exist?   ...Page 121
The Nature and Ministry of Angels   ...Page 121
Angels Minister to God   ...Page 122
Angels Minister to Christ   ...Page 122
Angels Minister to You and Me   ...Page 123
The Other Side: Satan   ...Page 123
Demons Who Attack Us   ...Page 124
Summary   ...Page 126

X. Walk in Fellowship
Ecclesiology - Fellowship in the Church
Preface   ...Page 133
The Local Church   ...Page 134
The Universal Church   ...Page 134
Foundations of the Church   ...Page 135
Distinctives of the Church   ...Page 137
Functions of the Church   ...Page 138
Leaders of the Church   ...Page 142
Organization of the Church   ...Page 145
Government in the Church   ...Page 145
Ordinances of the Church   ...Page 146
Baptism   ...Page 148
Dunk or Sprinkle?   ...Page 149
Summary   ...Page 150

XI. Walk in God's Image
Creationism - In the Beginning, God
Preface   ...Page 155
Early Beliefs   ...Page 158
Natural Theology   ...Page 159
Human Evolution   ...Page 160
Intelligent Design   ...Page 160
Theistic Evolution   ...Page 162

Christian Creationism   ...Page 163
Young Earth and Old Earth   ...Page 163
So, Which Theology Is Right?   ...Page 169

XII. Walk to the Future
Eschatology - All good things come to an end
Preface   ...Page 173
Death   ...Page 174
Jesus Did It All...   ...Page 175
Heaven   ...Page 176
Earth   ...Page 180
Hell   ...Page 182
The Return of Jesus and the Resurrection   ...Page 183
Life after Death   ...Page 184
The Judgment   ...Page 186
The Second Coming   ...Page 186
What Will Happen and When?   ...Page 187
Dispensational Premillennialism   ...Page 188
The Dispensations   ...Page 188
Historic Premillennialism   ...Page 192
Amillennialism   ...Page 194
Postmillennialism   ...Page 195
Signs of the Times   ...Page 197
The Antichrist   ...Page 198
The Revelation   ...Page 200
The 144,000   ...Page 200
So, Then, What Should We Believe?   ...Page 202

Epilogue   ...Page 205

Bible Translations   ...Page 207

How To Be Born-Again   ...Page 209

About the Author   ...Page 211

Foreword

"Theologians struggle to move from being obscure and over-detailed to being easily understood. Most can doubtless do a good job of presenting their basic doctrinal beliefs if given the time to do so.

"Buddy Merrick has done a fascinating and effective job in making serious and essential biblical doctrines simple and even entertaining… and to the point. New believers will have a real adventure that is exciting and edifying in these pages. It is not for the scholars, but for the people…like you and me.

"This book is reverent, clear and engaging. God will bless the sincere believer who enters into these pages to learn basic theological principles!"

Jimmy Draper
President Emeritus LifeWay

Prologue

Good Morning!

Let me ask you, why do you exist? Why do you take up space and suck up oxygen in this Big Clay House that God has built? What's the design? What's the purpose? Is there a Plan? And how does it all end? For you? For me? For that guy over there? And well, OK, for the whole world? Is there meaning behind it all?

My granddaughter, Little Brodie, sits on her Papa's lap. She looks up with her blonde baby hair and pretty little face and asks, "Papa Buddy, why am I me? Why wasn't I born a bug or a puppy?" Brodie has begun her first exploration into creationism, if not systematic theology, although she wouldn't put it that way.

Does God have a plan for me?

You see, Brodie's not interested in solving the scholarly queries of the ages. Nah, she's much more interested in whether Fluffy will make it to Heaven with her. She has no doubts about Heaven. She simply accepts it as a fact. Her faith is more absolute than the most academic dispensational premillennialist pretribulationist I've ever known, and it'll take a long time for any kind of titles like that to reach her vocabulary, if they ever do! Why can't our walk be as simple as that?

I've discovered, like millions of others, that soteriology, that is salvation, is the turning-point subject of a lifetime. Important? Goodness, yes! It's the pinnacle moment of our very lives! It's that day when we uncover The Truth: that a loving God actually planned that we could be free of the nasty sin-sickness that permeates this ol' world. To top it all off, as we accept that Truth, we also ensure our reservation in Brodie's Heaven, as she would say, "for ever and ever and ever."

It's a great plan. It required the sacrifice of the earthly life of God's beloved Son Jesus Christ to bring it about, but "it is finished" if we'll only receive Him.

Along the way, while we exercise our lungs and move about on this Big Blue Globe we call home, we mature in our Christian walk. We learn that Life isn't about how to survive the storm, but how to dance in the rain. We learn how God blesses us through His triune personalities, sends us angels, helps us individually and corporately, especially in our failures, and even gives us a glimpse of why it all started and how it all will end. That's what this book is all about.

Like every college student who ponders why he or she endured those long, taxing and even boring classes studying topics with long multi-syllabic names, I began to wonder if some really simple concepts they call "doctrines" could actually be explained without sounding like someone's been tenured too long in the ivy halls. So, I started to write.

OK, I admit some of this is a little deep for Brodie to understand, but I truly hope you'll enjoy clearing up some fuzzy ideas that have been nagging you for too long, and that your walk will be more fun and full after you "dig in" a little in this book. Hey, it's cool to grow a little, right?

Finally, it's also my fervent hope that one or two will peruse this book and wonder why it's taken so long for you to figure out that God loves you with an unfathomable love, and seeks to enjoy you - yes *you* - for all eternity, as His own. Maybe it's time you bowed your head and made a commitment to accept Jesus, to walk alongside Him, just like that ol' bellwether sheep on the cover of this book.

That'll change your life.

And, hey, deciding *not* to choose Jesus is, after all, still making a choice, right? And there's no downside for trying Jesus - the devil will always take you back! Even if you think that things are going OK, and you don't really need Jesus, remember, it wasn't raining when Noah built the ark. Things aren't always what they seem. Don't believe that? Try sitting in your parked car with sunglasses on and point a hair dryer at the passing cars. Betcha they slow down!

I can tell you that, on February 22, 1962, the day after attending a meeting of the Officers Christian Society in Pensacola, Florida, this Jersey boy of 19-years old, bowed my head while I was in the shower. Not very dramatic, huh? Yeah, well, at least it's a good place to be alone! There, I offered the worst sinner's prayer ever muttered. Almost word-for-word, I said, *"Lord* (off to a good start), *if You're all they crack you up to be, I'll give this a shot..."* and with that, I accepted Jesus as Messiah, Savior and Lord. Messiah, that He is the Son of God, the One whom God sent to save the world. Savior, that Jesus climbed that cross on Mount Calvary to pay the price for my sins, which I should have paid. And Lord, to whom I turned over my life for His leading, directing and blessing forever.

God confirmed our alliance. I was a Naval Aviation Cadet in the U. S. Navy. I doubt that those with whom I was serving thought that I was anything but the old Buddy, but very quickly I knew that my life had been radically changed. I had purpose. God had a plan and I was in it. I was useful in the overall cosmic-design of God the Creator. I wasn't just "right with God," it was so much more than that. I was one-on-one with Jesus, my new Friend, Mentor and Helper. We went everywhere together. And, I was never the same. It was like my eyes were seeing things I had never focused on before. For my ten cents worth of faith, maybe not even that much, God gave to me all the riches in Heaven, the pearly gates, the golden streets and joy unimaginable.

> *"No learning can make up for the failure to pray. No earnestness, no diligence, no study, no gifts will supply its lack."*
> *Edward McKendree Bounds (1835-1913)*

Jesus began right away. He taught me about happiness and about joy. He taught me how to work toward being righteous, like Him. He taught me about blessings, how to receive them and how to give them away. He taught me that, through it all, there is a reason, Brodie, that God created me to be me, and nobody else. It was good and I liked it. And He taught me how, in the final analysis, Jesus will literally take me by the hand and usher me to eternal enjoyment, and I will know all things as they really are.

God tells us to *"fix our eyes on Jesus, the author and perfecter of our faith"* (Hebrews 12:2), and I assure you, He's a much better author than I am. So, if He's in this book, which I pray that He is, then you should find it a very good read indeed.

One final thought: Before we even begin Chapter One: Walk In The Word, let's take just a moment and "Talk To God" before we try to "Walk With God." God hears prayers (Isaiah 30:19), God always responds to prayers (Psalm 5:7), and we can pray to God for grace, mercy and help (Hebrews 4:16), the Bible says.

Don't know how to pray? Use the acronym A.C.T.S.: Adoration (praise Him), Confession (own up to your sins that they may be forgiven and you can be clean, without sin), Thanksgiving (thank Him for what He's done for you, or what you trust He will do), and Supplication (tell Him what you need).

Jesus taught, *"If you, though you are evil, know how to give good gifts to your children, how much more will your Father in heaven give good gifts to those who ask him!"* (Matthew 7:11). All we need to do is ask!

Jesus says *"Ask and it will be given to you; seek and you will find; knock and the door will be opened to you"* (Matthew 7:7-8). What a promise!

Jesus, let me walk with you today. Let me wear the bell!

Feels good, doesn't it? So, come on with me now, and let's explore together a dozen ways to walk with God. They say, all who "Walk With God" will always reach their destination, but it's the journey that matters in the end.

Enjoy your trip!

You are loved,
Buddy
Rev. Dr. Meredith Samuel "Buddy" Merrick

1. Walk with the Word

Bibliology - The Bible, the Word of God

Preface

How accurate is the Bible?

Let's talk about that. Bibliology is the study of the Bible, the Word of God. The Bible is the inspired source of knowledge about God, Jesus Christ, the Holy Spirit, and our salvation and eternity along with all mankind. Without a clear understanding of the Bible, our views on these and other doctrines and issues become clouded and distorted, even subject to debate. 'Don't want that.

No wonder the Bible is the best-selling Book in the history of books.

The Bible is truly God's Word. From my own experience, some research, and the inspiration, guidance and counsel of the Holy Spirit in my own life, I know this to be true:

> *The Bible is truly God's Word. From my own experience, some research, and the inspiration, guidance and counsel of the Holy Spirit in my own life, I know this to be true.*

First, the basis of Christianity is found in the authority of Scripture. I once had a pastor who told me, *"Buddy, if someone tells you something and you are skeptical, find it in the Word. If you can find it, nail it down as a Bible truth. If you can't find it, take it with a grain of salt."*

That was some of the best counsel I've ever received. If you can't identify what is Scripture, then you can't properly distinguish any theological truth from error. That's logical, right? While there are different views as to what extent the Bible is inspired, there can be no doubt that the Bible itself claims that every word, in every part within its pages, every "jot and tittle" is inspired by God (I Corinthians 2:12-13; II Timothy 3:16-17). Among the proofs for the divine inspiration of the Bible are

>fulfilled prophecy,
>
>the unity of Scripture and
>
>the support of archeological findings.

Second, the Bible's most important proof is in the lives of those who read it, believe it and live it, according to its precepts. I'm a living testimony to that fact. The more I live as I understand how God wants me to live, the closer I get to Him, and the happier I am. Reading the Bible is one way God talks to me.

Third, bibliology teaches us that the Bible is inspired, meaning it's "breathed out" by God. A proper bibliology holds to the inerrancy of Scripture. No errors. The Bible doesn't contain any contradictions, or discrepancies or errors, and careful study will resolve any apparent differences. God used the personalities, styles and even the diverse vocations of more than forty human authors of Scripture to write the Bible, and even through all that, they still produced His Word to say exactly what He wanted to be said. The discovery of the Dead Sea Scrolls proved that the Bible is real and error-free! Wow!

If you're suffering with Truth Decay, brush up on your Bible!

Finally, for a Christian like me, and hopefully you, the Bible is Life itself. Its pages are filled with the very Spirit of God, revealing His heart and mind to us. What a wonderful and gracious God we have! He could have left us to struggle through life with no help at all, but instead He gave His Word to guide us, truly to be a *"lamp to my feet and a light to my path"* (Psalm 119:105). Truly pity the one who doesn't have the Bible as his companion, or a Bible to rely on as he walks in this world.

Like the marquis says, "If You're Suffering with Truth Decay, Brush up on Your Bible."

The Sixty-six Books

Dividing the Bible up into sections helps us remember where certain books are, and to some extent, even their content.

In the Old Testament, "the Law" is contained in the first five books of the Bible. This is also called the Jewish Torah, or the Pentateuch. These books are:

> Genesis: The beginnings
> Exodus: Deliverance of the Jews from slavery
> Leviticus: Laws and sacrifice
> Numbers: The earliest census and history
> Deuteronomy: Moses' writings

There are twelve "History" books that continue the story of the Israelites, including the conquest of the Promised Land, the judges and kings, the captivities and the return from exile:

> Joshua: The conquest
> Judges: The judges
> Ruth: Love and faith
> I Samuel: Samuel, Saul and David
> II Samuel: David, kingship and failure
> I Kings: Solomon, the temple and Elijah
> II Kings: Elisha and the fall of the kingdoms
> I Chronicles: David's reign
> II Chronicles: The kings of Judah
> Ezra: Reconstruction of the Temple
> Nehemiah: Rebuilding the walls of Jerusalem
> Esther: Redemption

There are five "Poetry" books which include wisdom works, hymns and proverbs.

> Job: Perseverance
> Psalms: Songs and poems

Proverbs: Wisdom works
Ecclesiastes: Life and obedience
Song of Solomon: Love and marriage

The Bible includes sections called "Major Prophets" and "Minor Prophets." The Major Prophet section is called that because those books are *longer*, not higher quality. The prophets were men who brought God's Word to the Israelites, including warnings of judgment, hope and predictions of the coming Messiah, Jesus. The section of Major Prophets includes five books:

Isaiah: Prophesy and judgment
Jeremiah: Prophesy and judgment
Lamentations: Poem of despair, a lament
Ezekiel: Sin, repentance and hope
Daniel: End times

The section of Minor Prophets includes 12 books:

Hosea: Unfaithful wife, unfaithful nation
Joel: Blessings and curses
Amos: Warning to seek God and live
Obadiah: Judgment
Jonah: Mercy
Micah: Confession and restoration
Nahum: Hope
Habakkuk: Praise
Zephaniah: Repentance
Haggai: Importance of the Temple
Zechariah: Hope
Malachi: Rewards for righteousness

The New Testament begins with four books called the "Gospels," the "good news" of the life of Christ. The "synoptic gospels," Matthew, Mark and Luke, are similar in their emphasis of Christ's humanity, while the Gospel of John reflects more of His deity. They are followed by the Acts, which records the missionary "actions" of the early followers of Jesus:

Matthew: Jesus the Son
Mark: Jesus the Servant

Luke: Jesus the Savior
John: Jesus the Messiah
Acts: The Holy Spirit

The Apostle Paul wrote 13 letters, the "Pauline Epistles," to young churches, encouraging and guiding them:

Romans: The Christian life
I Corinthians: Unity
II Corinthians: Power
Galatians: Justification
Ephesians: Grace, the gift of God
Philippians: Finishing the race
Colossians: Exhortations
I Thessalonians: Faith
II Thessalonians: Encouragement
I Timothy: False doctrine
II Timothy: Faithfulness
Titus: Encouragement
Philemon: Fairness

Eight "General Epistles" were written by other apostles and leaders:

Hebrews: Superiority of Christ
James: Faith without works
I Peter: Holiness
II Peter: False teachers
I John: Love and faith
II John: Heresy
III John: Loyalty
Jude: Heresy

The "Revelation" addresses seven churches in Asia Minor, modern day Turkey. The book of end times, it encourages us that God is in control and we're all part of His great plan.

Divine Origin of the Bible

The 39 Books of the Old Testament were written over a 1500-year period before the birth of Jesus. They were written primarily in Hebrew, with a few portions in Aramaic.

The 27 Books of the New Testament were written between roughly 50 and 100 AD, that is within 70 years of Christ's death and resurrection. The New Testament was written in Greek.

Translations of the Bible, such as the King James Version, are derived from existing copies of ancient manuscripts such as the Hebrew Masoretic Text (Old Testament) and the Greek Textus Receptus (New Testament), and are not interpretations of texts interpreted from other interpretations. The primary differences between today's Bible translations are simply how the translators interpret a word or sentence from the original language of the text source, Hebrew, Aramaic and Greek. Since words change as well as contemporary understanding of ancient languages, modern translations have been authored by dozens of eminent scholars, in a very sincere effort to translate the Bible into readable and understandable text, while still being very true to the Greek and Hebrew words. All the Scriptures in all the translations are virtually the same in their meaning.

The Origin of the Bible is God.

    It's an historical book that is backed by archeology.

    It's a prophetic book that has lived up to all of its claims.

It's God's letter to humanity, collected into 66 books written by 40 divinely inspired writers over a period of over 1,500 years. A careful and honest study of the biblical scriptures will show them to be true.

The Bible very powerfully validates its divine authorship through fulfilled prophecies. While an astonishing number of prophecies have been fulfilled, none have ever been proven false. That's extraordinary. Well, supernatural. God decided to use prophecy as His primary test of divine authorship, and an honest study of Biblical prophecy will compellingly reveal the supernatural origin of the Bible. No other holy book comes even close to the Bible in the amount of evidence supporting its credibility, authenticity and divine authorship.

The proof of the Bible is within the Scriptures themselves and by its authors:

The Bible Itself declares some 3,800 times, *"God said,"* or *"Thus saith the Lord"* (for example: Exodus 14:1; 30:1; Leviticus 4:1; Numbers 4:1; Deuteronomy 4:2; Isaiah 1:10; Jeremiah 1:11; Ezekiel 1:3 and more).[2]

Paul recognized that the things he was writing were the Lord's commandments (I Corinthians 14:37) and they were acknowledged as such by the believers (I Thessalonians 2:13).

Peter proclaimed the certainty of the Scriptures and the necessity of heeding the unalterable and certain Word of God (II Peter 1:16-21). And,

John also understood that his teaching was from God, and told his readers that to reject his teaching was to reject God (I John 4:6).

The authors used by God are diverse. Among the writers of the Scripture were:

>   Moses, a political leader;
>   Joshua, a military leader;
>   David, a shepherd;
>   Solomon, a king;
>   Amos, a herdsman and grower of sycamore figs;
>   Daniel, a prime minister;
>   Matthew, an unpopular tax collector;
>   Luke, a physician;
>   Paul, a government persecutor and then a Rabbi, and
>   Peter, an uneducated fisherman.

Few of these knew the others.

The Bible was written on three continents, Europe, Asia and Africa, from the desert, from prison, from the countryside, from the royal courts and from exile.

How's that for diversity?

Inspiration of the Bible

The Bible is the inspired Word of God, in the most absolute terms. The inspiration of the Bible is revealed:

in nature (Psalms 19:1-6),
in providence (Matthew 5:45),
in conscience (Romans 2:14-15),
in Christ Himself (John 1:18) and
in Scripture Itself (II Peter 1:21) as the *logos,* the Holy Word of God, and
in *Rhema,* the spoken, active and animated Word in my heart and yours.

In the "four-fours," Matthew 4:4 and Luke 4:4, Jesus says, *"Man does not live by bread alone, but by every word that proceeds from the mouth of God."* Words to live by!

The same Holy Spirit that is in you and me, also performed as the Guide over the Bible writers to guarantee that the Word would be error-free. The great Reformed leader, Benjamin B. Warfield, said, *"Inspiration is, therefore, usually defined as a supernatural influence exerted on the sacred writers by the Spirit of God, by virtue of which their writings are given Divine trustworthiness."*[3]

God the Holy Spirit indeed so influenced the writers that the Bible is created to be completely God's Word and totally human-error free. This inspiration of the Word extends to the very words selected by the writers and scribes and the Word of God which we use today is, in all essence, exactly as it was originally created.

Exactly.

Awesome!

The Bible Is Affirmed by Christ

Jesus Himself affirmed that *"not the smallest letter or stroke would pass from the Law until it would be fulfilled,"* clearly including the entirety of the Old Testament (Matthew 5:17-18).

In Luke's account, Jesus reminded His disciples that all things written about Him in the law of Moses, the prophets and the Psalms *"must be fulfilled"* (Luke 24:44).

When Jesus debated with the unbelieving Jews concerning His

right to be called the Son of God, Jesus referred them to Psalms 82:6 and reminded them that *"the Scripture cannot be broken"* (John 10:35).

In John 16, Jesus affirmed not only the inspiration of the Holy Spirit in the Old Testament but in the New Testament as well.

The Bible Is Affirmed by Paul

Paul affirms the inerrancy of the Bible. In I Timothy 5:18, Paul refers to Scriptures in Deuteronomy and Luke, affirming that the New Testament was as much the inspired Word as the Old Testament. In I Timothy 3:16, Paul tells us that Scripture is *"inspired by God."* In the Greek, his comments are translated *"breathed by God,"* thus adding credence to the inerrancy as well as inspiration of the Bible.

The Bible Is Affirmed by Peter

Peter, too, affirms the inerrancy of the Bible. In II Peter 1:21, Peter tells us that no Scripture is produced as a result of human will, but instead it's the product of the superintending power of the Holy Spirit. That's clear enough. Peter identifies the Scripture as *"the prophetic Word"* (verse 19), as *"prophesy of Scripture"* (verse 20) and as *"prophesy"* in verse 21. He affirms that the Scripture has its origin with God and that, although men penned the words, they did so as they were carried along by the Holy Spirit.[4]

Inerrancy of the Bible

Even more widespread evidence exists for absolute reliability of the Bible.

Did you know that there are more than 14,000 existing Old Testament manuscripts and fragments copied throughout the Middle East, Mediterranean and European regions, that agree dramatically with each other? Astounding! In addition, these texts agree with the Septuagint version of the Old Testament, which was translated from Hebrew to Greek some time during the third century before Christ.

The Dead Sea Scrolls, roughly 900 documents discovered between 1946 and 1956, also provide phenomenal evidence for the reliability of the ancient transmission of the Jewish Scriptures (Old Testament). Some of these scrolls were written as many as 150 years before the arrival of Jesus Christ. Portions of Scripture were found from every Book of the Old Testament except Esther, in Hebrew, Aramaic and Greek. One scroll is inscribed in pure copper! Talk about an amazing discovery, these Dead Sea Scrolls, all because one sheep went astray (kind of prophetic, isn't it?).

The Hebrew scribes themselves, who copied the Jewish Scriptures, dedicated their lives to preserving the accuracy of the holy books. These Old Testament scribes went to extraordinary lengths to insure manuscript reliability and they had the ability to do so. They were highly trained and meticulously observed. They counted every letter, word and paragraph against master scrolls. A single error would require the immediate destruction of the entire text! Ouch! Talk about a lousy day at the office!

The manuscript evidence for the New Testament is also dramatic, with over 5,300 known copies and fragments in the original Greek, nearly 800 of which were copied well more than a thousand years ago. Some manuscript texts date to the early second and third centuries, with the time between the original autographs and our earliest existing copies being a remarkably short 60 years.

Interestingly, this manuscript evidence far surpasses the manuscript reliability of other ancient writings that we trust as authentic every day. Compared to the Bible are these ancient texts:

> Julius Caesar's *"The Gallic Wars"* (10 manuscripts remain, with the earliest one dating to 1,000 years after the original autograph);
>
> Pliny the Younger's *"History"* (7 manuscripts; 750 years elapsed);
>
> Thucydides' *"History"* (8 manuscripts; 1,300 years elapsed);

Herodotus' *"History"* (8 manuscripts; 1,300 years elapsed);
Sophocles (193 manuscripts; 1,400 years);
Euripides (9 manuscripts; 1,500 years); and
Aristotle (49 manuscripts; 1,400 years).[5]

Homer's *"Iliad,"* the most renowned book of ancient Greece, has 643 copies of manuscript support. In those copies, there are 764 disputed lines of text, as compared to 40 lines in *all* the New Testament manuscripts.[6]

In fact, many people are unaware that each of William Shakespeare's 37 plays (written in the 1600's) have gaps in the surviving manuscripts, forcing scholars to, as they say, fill in the blanks.

All this pales in textual comparison with the over 5,300 copies and fragments of the New Testament that, together, assure us that *nothing's been lost!* In fact, all of the New Testament except eleven verses can be reconstructed from the writings of the early church fathers in the second and third centuries.[7]

Internal and External Evidences

There are both internal and external evidences as well, that the Bible is truly God's Word.

The "internal evidences" are those things inside the Bible that testify of its divine origin.

The Bible's unity. It's one unified Book. Even though the Bible is really sixty-six individual books, written on three continents, in three different languages, over a period of approximately 1500 years, by more than 40 authors who came from many walks of life, the Bible remains one unified book from beginning to end without contradiction. Extraordinary! This unity is unique from all other books ever written. That's evidence of the divine origin of the words, as God moved men in such a way that they recorded God's Own words and nothing else.

The prophecies are all fulfilled. The Bible contains hundreds of detailed prophecies relating to the future of individual nations (including Israel), to the future of certain cities, to the future of mankind, and to the coming of One who would be the Messiah, the Savior of not only Israel, but all who would believe in Him all over the world. Unlike the prophecies found in other religious books, the Bible's prophecies are extremely detailed and have never failed to come true.

There are over three hundred prophecies concerning Jesus Christ in the Old Testament alone. Not only was it foretold where He would be born and what family He would come from, but also how He would die and that He would rise again on the third day.

There simply is no logical way to explain the fulfilled prophecies in the Bible other than by God's divine origin. There is no other religious book with the extent or type of predictive prophecy of the Bible. The Bible is real, it's God's Word, and we can count on it!

The Bible has authority and power. Countless lives have been transformed by the supernatural power of God's Word. Drug addicts are cured by it, homosexuals are set free by it, derelicts and deadbeats are transformed by it, hardened criminals are reformed by it, sinners are rebuked by it, and by reading it, hate has been turned to love throughout ages. *Rhema* does its work.[10] The Bible possesses this transforming power because it is truly God's Word.

There's no way the Bible could do all it does unless it was written by God.

There are also "external evidences" that indicate the Bible is truly the Word of God.

It is historically accurate. Through archaeological evidences and other writings, the historical accounts of the Bible have been proven time and time again to be accurate and true. In fact, all the archaeological and manuscript evidence supporting the Bible makes it the best documented book from the ancient world. The fact that the Bible accurately and truthfully records historically verifiable events is a great indication of its truthfulness when dealing with religious subjects and doctrines. The Bible record helps substantiate its claim that it is the very Word of God. There's no way the Bible could do all it does, unless it was written by God!

It's authors were genuine. God used men from many walks of life to record His words to us. They were good men. They were honest and sincere men. They were willing to die often excruciating deaths for what they believed in. The men who wrote the New Testament and many hundreds of other believers (I Corinthians 15:6) knew the truth of their message because they had seen and spent time with Jesus Christ after He had risen from the dead. The transformation of seeing the risen Christ had a tremendous impact on them. They went from hiding in fear to being willing to die for the message God had revealed to them. Their lives and deaths testify to the fact that the Bible truly is God's Word.

The Bible is indestructible. From early Roman Emperors like Diocletian, through communist dictators and on to modern day atheists and agnostics, the Bible has withstood and outlasted all of its attackers and is still the most widely published book in the world today, the best-seller of all time.

Throughout time, skeptics have regarded the Bible as mythological, but archeology has established it as historical. Opponents have attacked its teaching as primitive and outdated, but its moral and legal concepts and teachings have had a positive influence on societies and cultures throughout the world.

The Bible is real, it's God's Word, and we can count on it!

Even to this very moment, it's still attacked by science, psychology, and political movements, and yet it remains just as true and relevant today as it was when it was first written. That relevance stands as a clear testimony that the Bible is truly God's Word and is supernaturally protected by Him.

Jesus said, *"Heaven and earth will pass away, but my words will never pass away"* (Mark 13:31). After looking at the evidence one can say without a doubt that yes, the Bible is truly God's Word, and it'll never pass away. And, that's a very good thing.

Through it all, the Bible is God's Word that will stand the test of time, whether we read it in the King James Version or a new "contemporary English" translation. The Truths in the Words are for all ages. II Timothy 3:16-17 tells us, *"All Scripture is God-breathed and is useful for teaching, rebuking, correcting and training in righteousness, so that the man of God may be thoroughly equipped for every good work."* That should about settle it!

Canonicity of the Bible

A biblical "canon" is a list of books considered to be authoritative scripture by a particular religious community.

How were books in the Bible deemed to be Scripture? Well, a key verse to understanding the process and purpose, and perhaps the timing of the giving of Scripture, is Jude 3 which states that a Christian's faith *"was once for all entrusted to the saints."* Since our faith is defined by Scripture, Jude is essentially saying that Scripture was given once for the benefit of all Christians.

The Bible is full, and complete. How comforting is it to know that there are no missing manuscripts yet to be found, there are no secret books only familiar to a select few, and there are no people alive who have special revelation requiring us to trek up some foreign land in order to be enlightened? The truth is, the same supernatural power God used to produce His Word has also been used to preserve it.

Plus, Psalm 119:160 tells us that all of God's Word is truth. When clear contradictions come up, in Scripture or in life, the Bible can be trusted.

Which books belong in the Bible? The early church had some very specific "criteria" in order for books to be considered as part of the New Testament. These included questions like:

> Was the book written by someone who was an eyewitness of Jesus Christ?
>
> Did the book pass the "truth test"? (i.e., did it concur with other, already agreed-upon Scripture?).
>
> Did it demonstrate a specific knowledge of such things as the true nature of God, the origin of the universe and life, the purpose and meaning of life, the wonders of salvation, and future events (including the destiny of mankind)?

These are things beyond what man can see with the natural eye, and think of with his mind, even beyond science as we know it.

The Word of God, as we have observed for all these centuries, explains to us everything we need to know of Christ (John 5:18; Acts 18:28; Galatians 3:22; II Timothy 3:15).

The Bible teaches us, corrects us, and instructs us into all righteousness, says II Timothy 3:16.

In 90 AD, the Council of Jamnia publicly recognized the Old Testament Canon, using specific "tests" for canonicity as inspired by God. To be included in the Old Testament, a text would require:

>an indication of divine authorship;
>
>a reflection of God speaking though a mediator (e.g., Exodus 20:1; Joshua 1:1; Isaiah 2:1);
>
>evidence that the human author was indeed a spokesman of God or a true prophet (e.g., Deuteronomy 31:24-26; I Samuel 10:25; Nehemiah 8:3);
>
>certain historical accuracy.

The books of the Old Testament were both divinely inspired and authoritative, and therefore were "canonical" at the moment they were written. Scripture was Scripture when the pen touched the parchment. The people recognized the writers as spokesmen from God.

Finally, there was a collection of books into a canon.[8] The Council of Hippo (AD 367) recognized the twenty-seven books of the New Testament and the Council of Carthage four years later affirmed that only those canonical books were to be read in the churches[9]. There were certain "tests" to determine New Testament canonicity as well:

>apostolicity of the author, therefore his authority;
>
>acceptance of the church at large;
>
>content consistency with doctrine;
>
>a reflection of inspiration.

The Apocrypha and Pseudepigrapha are examples of works which didn't meet this test, and beginning in 1640 AD, these texts were removed from most Protestant versions of the Bible. Catholic versions still include it.

Summary

For anyone who's been born again, there's an important theological point that any personal testimony of bibliology shouldn't miss. God has used the Bible, His Word, for all these ages for the single purpose of revealing Himself to you and me, and to communicate all things to all mankind just as He has done to us.

Ultimately, a study in bibliology clearly shows, over and over, that the church councils didn't decide if a book was Scripture, God did.

> God alone chose the human author and directed him when and what to write.
>
> God alone guided the early church councils in their recognition of the canon.

God alone created The Bible.

Way beyond the natural observational and scientific ability of mankind are the bibliology of such things as the true nature of God, the origin of the universe and life, the purpose and meaning of life, the wonders of salvation and even future events including the destiny of mankind.

The Word of God, valued and personally applied throughout the centuries by Christians like you and me, is sufficient to explain to us everything we need to know of Christ, to teach us, correct us, and instruct us into all righteousness.

Only God can reveal the Bible to us!

What a Great Gift the Bible is!

Surely, it's true beyond debate that *"All scripture is given by inspiration of God and is profitable for doctrine, for reproof, for correction, for instruction in righteousness, that the man of God be perfect, thoroughly furnished unto all good works"* (II Timothy 3:16-17).

Through the Grace of God, let it be so for every man and woman of God.

Three brothers left home for college, and they became very successful doctors and lawyers and prospered. Some years later, they chatted after having dinner together. They discussed the gifts they were able to give their elderly mother who lived far away in another city.

Milton, the first, said, "I had a big house built for Mama."

Marvin, the second, said, "I had a hundred thousand dollar theater built in the house."

Melvin, the third, said, "You know how Mamma loved reading the Bible and you know she can't read anymore because she can't see very well. Well, I met this preacher who told me about a parrot that can recite the entire Bible. It took twenty preachers twelve years to teach him. I had to pledge to contribute $100,000 to his church, but it was worth it. Mamma just has to name the chapter and verse and the parrot will recite it."

The other brothers were impressed.

After the holidays Mom sent out her Thank You notes. She wrote: "Milton, the house you built is so huge I live in only one room, but I have to clean the whole house. Thanks anyway."

"Marvin, you gave me an expensive theater with Dolby sound, it could hold 50 people, but all of my friends are dead, I've lost my hearing and I'm nearly blind. I don't think I'll ever use it. Thank you for the gesture; just the same."

"Dearest Melvin," she wrote, "you were the only son to have the good sense to give a little thought to your gift. The chicken was delicious. Thank you so much!"

The point is, only God can reveal the Bible to us. A parrot will never do!

If someone has not read the Bible much lately, I'd recommend it. It's a good read, it's user-friendly, and churches all over America offer tech support!

After one examines all the evidence, the simple and accurate conclusion is that the Bible is real, enduring, true, trustworthy and everything God said it would be. On that Foundation, and only that Foundation, we can confidently continue our study of 12 Ways To Walk With God. Come on, let's have some fun!

Praise God for His Word!

1. Rev. Charles Jolly, Madison Baptist Church, 203 Green Avenue at Shunpike Road, Madison, NJ 07940, 1979.

2. Enns, Paul, *The Moody Handbook of Theology*, (Chicago: Moody Publishers, 2008), pg. 156.

3. Warfield, B. B., *The Inspiration and Authority of the Bible* (Philadelphia: Presbyterian and Reformed, 1948), pg. 131.

4. Young, Edward J., *Thy Word Is Truth* (Grand Rapids: Eerdmans, 1957), pg. 25.

5. Geisler, Norman L. And Nix, William E., *A General Introduction To the Bible* (Chicago: Moody, 1986). pg. 367.

6. Ibid.

7. Ibid.

8. Guthrie, D., *The Zondervan Pictorial Encyclopedia of the Bible*, 5 vols. (Grand Rapids: Zondervan, 1975), 1:560.

9. Harrison, Everett F., *Introduction to the New Testament* (Grand Rapids: Eerdmans, 1964), pp. 103-106.

10. The word, *rhema* is used in Bible study to signify Jesus Christ's utterance. Both *rhema* and *logos* are translated into English as *"word,"* however, *"rhema"* is at times expressed as "a word from the Word," referring to the revelation received by the reader from the Holy Spirit when the Word (*logos*) is read. The Bible was originally written using 11,280 Hebrew, Aramaic and Greek words, but the typical English translation uses only around half that amount of words. Because the meanings of words in the original languages can't always be duplicated in English, this book, *12 Ways To Walk With God*, uses several translations, depending on which seems to be the clearest for that application.

II. Walk in the World

Anthropology - Why are we here anyway?

Preface

"Man's way leads to a hopeless end. God's way leads to an endless hope."

Little Brodie asked, "Why am I me?"

For the answer, we look into anthropology, to sort out the role of man from a biblical standpoint. The term "anthropology" comes from two Greek words, namely, *anthropos* meaning "man" and *logos* meaning "word, matter, or thing." So, a biblical anthropology is the study of man as understood primarily from Scripture.

> *God said, "Let us make man in our image, after our likeness; and let them have dominion…"*
> *Genesis 1:26*

Thus it often involves an examination of:
- your ancestors and mine in the creation of man,
- man in the "image of God,"
- the constitutional nature of man, and
- man after the fall. Of course, that means wo-man as well.

Other areas of anthropology concern include human dignity, freedom, depravity, culture, and society. So that's a lot.

Origin of Man

There are a myriad of views by people over the centuries concerning the origin of man. Some insist that God, in an act of divine fiat, simply created everything (Genesis 1:1). Some hold to atheistic evolution, suggesting that God began the process all right, but that He did it through evolution.

This "atheistic evolution" began with Charles Darwin, who proposed that a combination of atoms, motion, time and pure chance evolved all that exists. In Darwin's <u>Origin Of The Species</u>, he argued the following:

> Variation is the reason for some offspring to be superior to their parents;
>
> Survival of the fittest;
>
> A struggle for existence eliminates the weaker, less fit varieties;
>
> Better qualities emerge through heredity, and;
>
> New species come into existence by this method, after the passage of sufficient time.[1]

Of course, if Darwin's right, then there's no God, no divine creation and no reason for morality. That doesn't work for me and it should be no good for you, either.

"Theistic evolution" is the teaching that plants, animals and man gradually evolved from lower forms (monkeys included), but that God supervised the proceeding.[2] Well, here, too, if this theory is correct, then Adam was not the first person and that analogies between the firstborn man and Christ in Romans 5:12-21 are meaningless. God's Word tells us that it was He who created us, in His image and His likeness, and that statement disputes that we evolved from anything other than God. I believe God, so the theology of theistic evolution doesn't work for me either. I refuse to believe that I emanated from a bug or a chrysanthemum!

"Progressive creationism" rejects a literal six-day creation. It teaches that the days of creation are not literally 24-hour periods, but ages, which harmonizes somewhat with the scientific teaching of antiquity with the Bible account. A "gap theory" supposes a lengthy period of time between the first and second day of creation to accommodate science. Ahh, still not convinced.

In the so-called "fiat creation," God created the heavens and the Earth in six days, literally (and rested on the seventh day). Why not? God is certainly capable of doing that, and all geological formations can be explained through the flood of Noah.[3] The basis for the twenty-four-hour creation is the Bible account of Genesis in the first two chapters:

> God created man out of dust and Christ affirmed His creation as truth (Matthew 19:4).
>
> God created man and woman (Genesis 1:27). "Created" means they didn't evolve.
>
> God created in six 24-hour periods. (Genesis 1:5, 8, 13, 19, 23 and Exodus 20:9-11).
>
> God created us to be unique.
>
> We have morals and sensitivity and accountability.
>
> We have a soul and we are eternal.
>
> We are made in God's image and God delights in us.

The Holy Spirit affirms all that in our being, and that we are right in our faith.

There are several other points that can be made from the Genesis narrative regarding the creation of man, so let's look at them, too:

First, the origin of man isn't in "naturalistic evolution," but in the mind of God. Man wasn't some kind of an afterthought or the result of blind evolutionary forces, but was created according to a very specific purpose, plan and good pleasure of God. In Genesis 1:26, God says *"let us make man in our image..."* The *"our"* in that statement obviously refers to the Trinity: God the Father, God the Son, and God the Holy Spirit.

Second, man is the pinnacle of creation. Again, we are made in the image of God. Nothing else, including the angels, is said to be made in the image of God. That makes us very unique in the created order. Because of that uniqueness, that creation, we're both privileged and responsible. Of course. We reflect the image of God.

Third, God continues, *"...and our likeness."* We bear a special relationship to God. In our original creation, coming from the hand of God, we were holy, upright, and perfect and there was no hostility between God and us. A holy God can create nothing but that which is holy.

Fourth, we have a certain role in creation. We were created to rule over God's earth, that is, to have dominion over it, God says.

Finally, man was created in what appears as an instantaneous act of God, bringing together material aspects and God's breath of life. God breathed His Character in us! Wow! We were not taken from some previously existing animal. Our creation gives rise to the dual nature of our experience as we exist in both a spiritual (heavenward) and material (earthward) direction. No other animal has those qualities. Man - God-breathed - is unique!

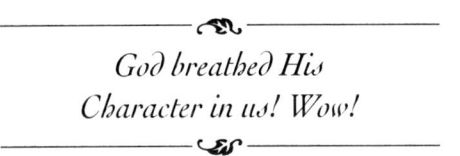

> *God breathed His Character in us! Wow!*

The Material Part of Man

The Bible tells us about this dual residency in II Corinthians 5:1, in our earthly house and in an eternal building of God, the distinction between the material (body) and the non-material (soul and spirit).

The body is the prison house of the soul.[4] It's formed of dust and will return to dust at death. The practice of Hedonism views the body as the only important part of man. Many today believe *"if it feels good, do it."* That's not only bad advice, it's a complete denial of the soul. Jesus refutes this philosophy, too, affirming the value of the soul as distinct from the body.

So, the body is the partner of the soul. I have a good Mormon friend who shames me with his lifestyle of obedience and especially his belief that the body is the temple of the Lord (I Corinthians 6:19-20). Ralph drinks orange juice when I order coffee, as his means of glorifying God. I so often indulge my body rather than mastering it, submitting it to

God as I'm commanded to do (Romans 12:1). I love a pepperoni pizza, even if it doesn't love me. I need to work on that. Or, eat out more often with Ralph and eat what he eats.

The Apostle Paul said, *"I do all things for the sake of the gospel, that I may become a fellow partaker of it. Do you not know that those who run in a race all run, but only one receives the prize? Run in such a way that you may win. And everyone who competes in the games exercises self-control in all things. They then do it to receive a perishable wreath, but we an imperishable. Therefore I run in such a way, as not without aim; I box in such a way, as not beating the air; but I buffet my body and make it my slave, lest possibly, after I have preached to others, I myself should be disqualified"* (I Corinthians 9:23-27).[5] We must master our material man as well.

The Nonmaterial Part of Man

When God created man in His image, He created man in His spiritual image, because God does not have a body. Therefore, man was created in God's Spiritual image. That makes sense. How? In our spirit:

God created in us a freedom to choose. God created us with an intellect, a self-consciousness and self-determination that allows us to make choices and frankly, it's this human quality that enables a person to indeed accept or deny redemption in Christ.

God created us with a spiritual side. God is a Spirit. He created Man with a soul and a spirit. Because of his spirit, man is a rational, moral, free agent, and thereby distinguished from all other forms of life. Man belongs to the same order of being as God Himself. That's why we are capable of communicating with God the Creator. We can know God.

God created us with a moral nature. Our "self" was created in original righteousness. That righteousness was lost in the Fall of Man, but was restored to those who will receive Him by the sacrificial death and resurrection of Christ. Ephesians 4:24 emphasizes that the new self of the believer is *"in the likeness of God [and] has been created in* righteousness and holiness." Colossians 3:10 declares that the new self is *"being renewed to a true knowledge according to the image of the One who created him,"* a reference to Genesis 1:26. Being born "anew" is a good way of putting it.

The Origin of the Soul

There are numerous theories of the origin of the soul, such as the theory of preexistence supported by Hinduism, Plato, Philo and Origen. Also, the Traducian theory of William G. T. Shedd postulates that the soul as well as the body is generated by the parents. Christians, however, believe that our human soul is an immediate and individual creation by God alone.[6] That is to say that

> our body was propagated by our Mom and Dad, and it'll die, but
>
> our soul was created by God, to live eternally. This view is supported by Baptists, Roman Catholics and Reformed Christians as well.

They also believe that man is a dichotomous being, that is a two-part being, consisting of body and soul. Soul and spirit are interchangeable as affirmed by the Genesis 2:7 account of man who was born of dust and became a living soul (Job 27:3). Body and soul (or spirit) together are also mentioned as constituting the entire person in Matthew 10:28, I Corinthians 5:3 and 3 John chapter 2.

Fall of Man

The story of Adam and Eve is historical, not allegorical. If Adam wasn't a real creature who brought sin into human existence, then Jesus' existence and atonement is unnecessary. Christ's own testimony in Matthew 19:3-5, however, attests that the account of Adam and Eve is indeed an historical event, and Adam and Ever were real people.

Adam and Eve were tested by God in three areas: the lust of the flesh, the lust of the eyes and the boastful pride of life (I John 2:16). They were tempted and deceived by Satan.

Ladies take note: It was to Adam that God gave the commandment (Genesis 2:17, *"But of the tree of knowledge of good and evil, thou shalt not eat of it..."*). Eve only heard of it from her husband second-hand. Note how she even recites it wrong in 3:3.

It was also Satan's lie that they wouldn't die. They did die, spiritually. Satan, the serpent, told them they'd be like God, knowing good and evil, but he didn't tell them about the pain, suffering and death that would occur through their sin. Eve was deceived, but Adam had been told directly by God first-hand and knew the command well. It was Adam who actually chose to disobey God.

As a result of sin, God made a judgment on the woman. She would suffer pain in childbirth, and her husband would rule over her (Genesis 3:16).

As a result of sin, God made a judgment on the man. He would toil for food and would eventually die and return to dust (Genesis 3:17-19).

As a result of sin, God made a judgment on the whole human race. All are subject to death. You and me as well. But, praise God, there is redemption for all who will confess and believe on Jesus as their Savior and Lord. Satan, where is your victory, death where is your sting? We are victorious over death and sin, by the Blood shed for us.

> *Jesus said to His Father, "I pray not that thou shouldst take them out of the world, but that thou shouldst keep them from the evil... as thou hast sent me into the world, even so have I also sent them into the world."*
> *Jesus Christ, in John 17:15 and 18*

Summary

Life can be defined in 5 T's:

Life is a <u>T</u>est. Since the time of Adam and Eve, God continues to test us, individually. Sometimes we fail and must try again. Sometimes we succeed. God is pleased and gives us another test.[7]

Life is a <u>T</u>rial. I don't know why some trials come upon us, but I do know that no trial comes without God's permission and His subsistence to deal with it. In a born-again Christian's life, all trials have meaning and purpose.

Life is a Temp job. My parents birthed a boy who will live three score and ten, and maybe a few more years by the grace of God (Psalms 90:10), but my soul was created by God to live eternally with Him, and I will. God also built in me a spirit as a means with which to connect to the Father, Son and Holy Spirit. When I became committed to Jesus, and He responded to me, the Holy Spirit connected to my spirit, and from that moment, I have what the world calls a "direct connection" to God, and He to me.

> *Life's not a journey to the grave with the intention of arriving safely in a pretty and well-preserved body, but rather to skid in broadside thoroughly used-up, totally worn-out and loudly proclaiming, "Wow, what a ride!"*

Life is a Training ground. We know only a little bit of what Heaven is like or what will be the occupation of our eternity. But, we can surely be confident that God continues to train us, every day, for His service here and His glory there.

Life is a Transition. It is very clear that we were beautifully created to eternally glorify our beloved Maker. Don't like yourself? Change your mind. God loves you just the way you are.

It's so exciting to know that we're not just evolved. We were created by a loving God who loved us so much He gave His son for us, and that He created us not just to live a few years on Earth, but to live eternally. Someone once said, "Life's not a journey to the grave with the intention of arriving safely in a pretty and well-preserved body, but rather to skid in broadside, thoroughly used-up, totally worn-out and loudly proclaiming, 'Wow, what a ride!'"

Man's way leads to a hopeless end, but God's way leads to an endless hope. We were created for eternity. We are fearfully and wonderfully made (Psalms 138:14) in God's Matchless Plan.

>   *A* lthough things are not perfect,
>   *B* ecause of trial or pain,
>   *C* ontinue in thanksgiving,
>   *D* o not begin to blame.

E ven when the times are hard, and
F ierce winds are bound to blow,
G od is forever able,
H old on to what you know.
I magine life without His love,
J oy would cease to be,
K eep thanking Him for all the things that
L ove imparts to thee.
M ove away from temptations' snare,
N o weapon that is known,
O n Earth can yield the power that
P raise can do alone!
Q uit looking at the future,
R edeem the time at hand,
S tart every day with worship,
T o 'thank' is a command.
U ntil we see Him coming
V ictorious in the sky,
W e'll run the race with gratitude,
X alting God most high,
Y es, there'll be good times and yes some will be bad, but
Z ion waits in glory...where none are ever sad!

"This world is not my home I'm just passing through.
My treasures are laid up somewhere beyond the blue.
The angels beckon me from Heaven's open door
And I can't feel at home in this world anymore.
O Lord you know I have no friend like you,
If Heaven's not my home then Lord what will I do?
The angels beckon me from Heaven's open door
And I can't feel at home in this world anymore."[8]

For many years, this little country folk song by Albert E. Brumley was sung by *Buddy Merrick & Praise* in concert. I still sing it, albeit mostly to myself now while I wander through the 5 T's of Life. I still believe it as I look forward to our heavenly home where I'll be with the Lord forever.

Boxer George Foreman once said, *"I don't even think about a retirement program because I'm working for the Lord, for the Almighty. And even though the Lord's pay isn't very high, his retirement program is, you might say, out of this world!"*

Amen, brother George, amen.

---

[1] Coder, S. Maxwell and Howe, George F., *The Bible, Science, and Creation* (Chicago: Moody, 1965), pp. 60-61.

[2] Culp, C. Richard, *Remember Thy Creator* (Grand Rapids: Baker, 1975), pg. 148.

[3] The work of Whitcomb and Morris, *The Genesis Flood,* remains a hallmark for study on this subject.

[4] Chafer, Lewis Sperry, *Systematic Theology,* 3 viols. (Dallas: Dallas Seminary, 1947) 2:146. This was the view of the Greek philosophers who placed a great dichotomy between body and soul. The soul was nonmaterial and good; the body was material and evil.

[5] When Paul wrote these words to the Christians in Corinth, Greece, he could surely assume that they all knew about the Olympic Games that took place in Greece every four years from 776 BC until they were suppressed by the Emperor Theodosius in AD 393. His words still ring true, and they still witness alongside the Olympics played worldwide today.

[6] Shedd, William G. T., *Systematic Theology,* 3 viols. (Reprint, London: Clarke, 1960), 2:146.

[7] I learned the concept that *"life is a test"* from Rick Warren in his book, *The Purpose-Driven Life* (Grand Rapids: Zondervan, 2002), pg. 42ff. Life really is a test, isn't it?

[8] Brumley, Albert E., Clearbox Rights, LLC, 1937. An old country folk song, sung often in concert by *Buddy Merrick & Praise.* Used by permission.

III. Walk Away from Sin

Hamartiology - Sin and What it Does to Us

Preface

"Christ Jesus came into the world to save sinners...the worst of them."

NEWTOWN, CT, Friday morning, December 14, 2012: A 22-year-old mentally-ill man-boy kills his mom (early in the morning ostensibly before she would leave for work). He dresses himself in combat gear, and drives to the local elementary school. Once inside, he proceeds to the classroom of 6-year-old first-grade kids, and opens fire with three semiautomatic weapons. He kills 20 kiddies and 6 teachers who try to stop him.

Why does this happen?

A psychiatrist on Fox News said simply, "Because he is spiritually dead."

Another said, "In this state of mind, he knew he was never going to come back to his home, so he acts out a final gruesome act, like a video game, to illustrate how troubled he is."

And then he apparently shoots himself, ending it all.

Why does this happen? Because sin has taken God's creation and turned it against everything and anything good, seeking to display evil, as evil as evil can be.

This is not God's Plan. Yet, God knew, when Adam and Eve fell in the Garden of Eden, that, having given man the privilege of free choice, only man could choose between sin and goodness. God could lead and direct and guide. God could produce examples throughout history. God could cajole and urge, plead and cry to man to repent, as an individual and corporately. But only man can choose.

God will come again to the world in the Person of Jesus, His Son, according to John 14:3.

Satan, the Prince of this World, and of the Power of Sin, will finally be defeated. Satan does not have infinite power. He is still accountable to God as seen in the story of Job. Christ has won victory over Satan for all who place their trust in Jesus. In his judgment, Satan not only fell from his exalted position, but his defeat by Christ was ultimate and he was rendered powerless through the Cross. The Bible says he will be cast out of Heaven during the tribulation (Revelation 12:13), bound in the pit for a thousand years (Revelation 20:2-3), and finally be cast in the lake of fire for eternity (Revelation 20:7-10).

On the cross, Christ conquered sin, as every born-again Christian knows. Christ will return one day, *"like a thief in the night,"* and He will reign over a sinless world once again as it was in the beginning. Then, Jesus will usher in eternity.

Sin will be no more.

The horror of sin was displayed in one last elementary school play, starring 20 innocent little boys and girls. If this sin doesn't affect a person, then that person is as cold as a 22-year-old with no reason to live, and he or she needs Jesus perhaps more than any person in the entire world. Nothing can help that person but prayer and a merciful savior. Hitler is not alone in infamy.

Why is sin so bad? Why is sin so hard to avoid?

They say, *"If you do not want to reap the fruits of sin, stay out of the devil's orchard."*

Sin? Who wants to study about sin? Yet, it's important, for if one doesn't know the nature of sin, how can one guard against it, or even confess it and obtain forgiveness? The word for sin that is used most frequently in the Bible is *hamartia*, missing the mark, which is the root of the word harmartiology, the study of the doctrine of sin. Paul used the verb *hamartano* when he wrote, *"For all have sinned, and come short of the glory of God* (Romans 3:23)."

A church marquis once read: *"The wages of sin is death. Repent before payday."* That's pretty good.

While few would argue with the logic, one might ask, what is sin, anyway? Sin is...

>...our transgressing of the law of God (Romans 2:23, 5:14 and Galatians 3:19).

>...our failure to conform to the standard of God, to either miss the mark, or walk in the opposite direction of what we should. All have fallen short.

>...our acts, and deeds, and our sin nature, a power that deceives us and leads us to destruction, were it not for the saving grace of Jesus Christ.[1]

>...our rebellion against God. We can love the Lord, and still find that our mind is sometimes without restraint (Matthew 24:12).

>...our wrongful acts toward God. Who of us has not failed to obey God's Ten Commandments (Exodus 20:1-11)? Who of us has not, at times, failed to live a righteous life (Exodus 20:12-17)? Who of us has not gone days without a single thought of Jesus or God, or the righteousness of our walk?

God has a high and holy standard of what is right (righteousness), and so long as we follow that divine standard we'll see ourselves as we truly exist in God's eyes. Do we do that? No, too often we want to create our own standards. Yet the Word of God tells us clearly that God has established the standard of righteousness we must attain for entry into Heaven, and we've all missed that mark. That's where Jesus comes in, praise God!

Know Sin. No God.
Know God. No Sin.

The shortest distance between a problem and a solution is the distance between our knees and the floor. The one who kneels to the Lord can stand up to anything. We need to pray.

Every one of us can be charged with the sin of the Pharisees, whom our Lord accused of leaving undone the things they ought to have done (Matthew 23:23; Luke 11:42). James 4:17 reads, *"Therefore to him that knoweth to do good, and doeth it not, to him it is sin."* Romans 14:23 tells us that *"whatsoever is not of faith is sin."* Wow, that's a super-tough standard!

When we fail to decide on actions on the basis of what we know is right, we deserve condemnation, because we didn't act according to our own conviction. As a result, we shortchange ourselves of God's blessings. To thine own self be true. You know what's right. Do it! God will reward you for it! Remember, the image of how you live your life may be the only Bible some people will ever read!

> *The image of how you live your life may be the only Bible some people will ever read!*

Original Sin

Let's understand that we're born into a sinful state and condition. Bummer! That sin is derived from the original root of the human race (Adam). It's present in the life of every individual from the time of his or her birth and it's the inward root of all the actual sins that defile the life of a person.[2]

Original sin is the corruption of our whole nature. That's not what we were designed for! We were designed for righteousness, the very righteousness of Jesus Christ, God's Son. We were designed for victory, victory, victory over every kind of sin. When God ordains, He sustains. For victory! Just like Jesus.

The result of that original sin is that man is totally depraved (the "T" in Calvin's TULIP). Total depravity does not mean that

    everyone is as thoroughly depraved in his actions as he could possibly be

        ("I'm not as bad as he is"), nor that

    everyone will indulge in every form of sin

        ("Well, I've never murdered anyone"), nor that

    a person can't appreciate and even do acts of goodness

("Why would God not allow a good person like me into Heaven?").

If we were so depraved, how then, in the natural, could a person ever please a demanding God? We'll get to that.

OK, so man has an innate sinful nature. The point is, every part of every person is affected, infected, with original sin:

> man's intellect (II Corinthians 4:4),
> his conscience (I Timothy 4:2),
> his will (Romans 1:28),
> his heart (Ephesians 4:18) and
> his entire being (Romans 1:18-3:20).

First John 2:16 says that Adam and Eve were tested by God in three areas:

> the lust of the flesh,
> the lust of the eyes and
> the boastful pride of life.

We're told in the Bible not to lust for things of the flesh, or to lust for things of the world. The world will lure a Christian into sin. The Bible tells us that Satan manifests himself in foolishness (I Corinthians 3:19), immorality (I Corinthians 5:10) and hostility toward God (James 4:4). That's where Satan lives!

When we were baptized, we demonstrated that we were crucified to those sins of Satan and the world, and raised to walk in a newness of life (Romans 12:1), shunning sin. Yet, we are tested every day.

We're told in the Bible that the flesh is the willing instrument of sin (Romans 7:18). The flesh is our natural capacity to leave God out of our life, like studying God's Word after forgetting to ask His blessing on that act. How many times do we do that?

How many times do we treat God like the rubber ball on that paddle where the ball is connected by a long rubber band? We smack that ball toward God, but before we give Him a chance to act on it, we jerk the paddle and draw it back to ourselves, as if we can handle the situation better than God can. Aw, come on, we've all done that. Foolish pride.

We're told in the Bible that the sinful flesh encourages lust and controls the mind (Ephesians 23). It governs the life of non-Christians (Romans 8:5-6). Let's understand that sin originates from the pits of Hell. It's Satan's deceit and so the devil has the unbeliever just where he wants him. Very sad.

We're told in the Bible that Satan is real, and that he seeks to destroy us and make us ineffective in our Christian life. Satan is the proponent of sin, and the opponent of any one who would live sinless. He's intent on devouring people like us (I Peter 5:8), so James 4:7 tells us to resist him, and Paul tells us to put on holy armor for a spiritual battle with him (Ephesians 6:10-17).

Sin (Satan) tells the non-Christian that he can handle life better than God can. Satan invented that paddle game we play. Sin makes the unbeliever timid about letting go and letting God. So, day after day, year after year, the unbeliever convinces himself that he doesn't need God, or that God isn't real, or that God can't help. Or, that he, the sinner, is just too unworthy for God to truly love him. Balderdash! God loves us all! And, God is eager to help. God doesn't call the qualified, He qualifies the called. Like the Army says, God will make a man "all he can be." Better than that - all you *should* be. That goes for ladies, too. Satan shouldn't get away with concealing that! We shouldn't let him!

The Punishment for Sin

God punishes sin, and that's not a bad thing. The first and primary reason God punishes sin is in order to prove Himself righteous and just. This justice may be hard to understand - impossible for the unbeliever - but remember, God punished sin most fully on the cross of Calvary (Romans 3:21-26; 9:19-23). Through that punishment, we were saved. Righteousness Personified. Good thing!

A second reason God punishes sin is to bring back an erring son or daughter or to deter others from sinning. Good thing!

Spiritual death, physical death, and eternal death, all three, are punishments for sin, as are certain sufferings in this life. Eternal death is, of course, the gravest punishment for sin imaginable. In this case,

God makes it impossible for the sinner, who dies apart from the saving mercy (unmerited forgiveness) and grace (unmerited favor) of Christ, to ever be reconciled with God. Torment will be his eternal lot. He will be eternally separated from God, *"shut out of the Lord's presence forever,"* as Paul says in II Thessalonians 1:8-9 (see also Matthew 25:41, 46). That's the very definition of terrible!

Sin always has consequences for both the present life as well as the next. While we can't escape consequences of sin in this life, or judgment for sin in the next, this judgment doesn't in any way revoke our salvation. No way! That'd be like revoking Jesus' work. We'll still be with the Lord forever, and our sin, although always regrettable, will never affect the nature of our relationship with Him. The Bible tells us that clearly in I Corinthians 3:10-15; II Corinthians 5:10 and Romans 14:10-12.

Be confident, we are saved from sin forever!

We Are Saved from Sin

God provides for us, in our heartfelt quest to battle all sin, with
> the Word of God,
>> the intercession of Christ (I John 2:1) and with
>> a personal indwelling of the Holy Spirit.

The Holy Spirit guides the believer in all things,
> anointing us (I John 2:20),
> sealing us (Ephesians 1:13, 4:30),
> empowering us (Acts 1:8),
> filling us with the very Spirit of God (Ephesians 5:18) and
>> enabling us to live as we want to live, for Christ, by the Spirit (Galatians 5:16).

So what's the remedy for sin in a Christian's life? Repent. How do we do that? Here are six ways to repent:

> One, be really sorry and declare your sin. Psalms 38:18 declares, *"For I will declare mine iniquity; I will be sorry for my sin."* Recognize that you've committed a sin. Feel true sorrow

12 Ways to Walk with God

for what you've done, for disobeying God and for any pain you may have caused somebody else.

Second, confess the sin to God. There's something supernaturally therapeutic about telling God, honestly, about your sin.

Third, ask God for his forgiveness. Then, forgive others who have hurt you. Remember, real forgiveness does not require remuneration. If you're looking for someone to tell you how wonderful you are for forgiving them, or for some kind of payback or reward, then it's not forgiveness. Likewise, God will not demand a bargain for His forgiveness, so don't offer one. Finally, forgive yourself.

> *Real forgiveness does not require remuneration.*

Fourth, rectify any problems caused by the sin, physical, mental, emotional, and spiritual damage. If it's impossible to fix the problem, sincerely ask forgiveness of those you wronged and then try to find another way to show your change of heart.

Fifth, truly forsake sin. Don't just cover them up to make yourself feel good. Proverbs 28:13 says, *"He that covereth his sins shall not prosper: but whoso confesseth and forsaketh them shall have mercy."* Make a promise to yourself and to God that you'll never again repeat the sin. If it happens again, repent again. Pretty simple. Be real about it.

Sixth, receive God's forgiveness. God will forgive you when you truly repent with a sincere heart. Receive God's forgiveness and know you are forgiven. When He does forgive you, be at peace with yourself and confident that you are clean. Don't hold onto your sin and the sorrow you've felt. Let it go, and thank God.

Finally, remember God. Faith is directly proportional to the number of times you can recall God acting in your life. Your victory over sin will edify and sustain you again and again. Wow, isn't that great?

By the way, God says, of the repentant Jews in Hosea 14:4, that *"I will heal their backsliding, I will love them freely: for mine anger is turned away from him."* If God helped them to stop their backsliding, loved them and turned his anger from them, how much more will he also do that for you and me? We can count on God!

Summary

Hamartiology, the study of sin, explains that we're all sinners, by inheritance, by imputation, and by our own personal choice. We all "miss the mark."

It shows us why God must condemn us for our sins. Hamartiology points to the solution for sin, the atoning sacrifice of Jesus Christ. When we truly come to grips with our sinful nature, we begin to fathom the depth and breadth of the nature of our great God who, on the one hand, condemns sinners to Hell in righteous judgment, then, on the other hand, satisfies His own requirement for perfection through the sacrificial Blood of His Only Son.

> *Only when we understand the depth of sin can we understand the height of God's love.*

Only when we understand the depth of sin can we understand the height of God's love for sinners. That's when accepting Jesus as Messiah, Savior and Lord really begins to make sense!

Once saved, we stand justified forever for all our sin, original sin and everyday sin (Romans 5:1). The Lord (as our Master) chastens us for our sin, but enjoys our confession and the progress we make toward living a sinless life as we mature spiritually. God's purpose for us is that we become more and more like Jesus, righteous and without sin. Though we will never reach sinless perfection in this life, living righteously is our goal. God is faithful to forgive and cleanse us (I John 1:9) and He does. Believe it, conceive it, take steps to achieve it. Then, leave the rest to God and

> *Believe it, conceive it, take steps to achieve it. Then, leave the rest to God and receive it!*

receive it!. Faith is not believing that God can, it's knowing that He will.

Here's a true story: I had a dream one night. I dreamed I had died and gone to Heaven. There I stood before God at the Judgment. Afraid, I began to express how sorry I was for all the sins I had committed in my life, and even began to get specific. In mid-sentence, the Father lovingly said, *"Buddy, I'm looking here in the Lamb's Book of Life, and all I see are blank pages with your name on them. They're all blank, except for this common inscription at the top of each page: 'Bought and paid for by the blood of the Lamb.'"* Then, with a smile, God said, *"Welcome home, my spotless son."*

Now, that might not be high-level theology, but it is an experience that changed my life, and I believe it's "spot-on" that I'm "spot-less" before the Maker, thanks to my redemption in Jesus.

In Jesus, we will know sin no more. Sin, where is your victory? We're overcomers, victorious over sin by the Blood of our Savior!

Believer 1, Satan zero. Final score!

---

[1] Arndt, William F. And Gingrich, Wilbur F, *A Greek-English Lexicon of the New Testament and Other Early Christian Literature*, 2nd ed., rev. F. Wilbur Gingrich and Frederick W. Danker (Chicago: University of Chicago, 1979), pg. 611.

[2] Ibid.

Three ways to Battle Sin
1. Read the Word
2. Let Christ intersead
3. rely on Holy Spirit

Jump up & claim Victory

[Handwritten notes: Roman Rd. 3:28, 6:23, 10:9+10; John 3:16; Redeemed, Reconciliation, Propitiation, Eph. 4:11-24; Justification, Sanctification; Regenerates]

IV. Walk Saved

Soteriology - All about Salvation, so Rich and Free

Preface

"Don't give up. Even Moses was once a basket case."

The jailer asked Paul in Acts 16:30, "What must I do to be saved?" He would have known if he'd looked into soteriology, the doctrine of salvation.

Christian soteriology is the study of how an individual is saved by grace through faith in Jesus Christ. OK, then it's also how a Christian is reconciled to the Triune God in spite of his or her sin and its resulting death, both physical and spiritual.

Within Christian soteriology, there's a wide range of debate surrounding the question: "Exactly how is an individual saved?" What roles are played by divine sovereignty versus human responsibility? Then too, is the question of the relationship between faith and works with regard to

    a) free-will,
    b) absolute moral law, and
    c) man's desperate need for salvation.

> *"Believe in the Lord Jesus and you will be saved, along with everyone in your household."*
> Acts 16:31 NLT

[Handwritten: Holy Spirit 1. convicts 2. Regenerates 3. Indwells 4. gifts 5. Seals]

39

The Bible tells us that salvation belongs to the Lord and is available to God's adopted sons and daughters.

> Salvation is bestowed by the grace of God on man.
>
> Salvation is unmerited. It's a gift of God, solely given because God loves us.
>
> Salvation is obtained through faith in Jesus Christ. It's totally free and not obtained by works.

The process of salvation includes the work of God the Father, God the Son and God the Holy Spirit, true, and there is, as well, a responsibility and role of the believer. Yes, the believer does have a role. The believer must acknowledge that Jesus is the Messiah the Son of God, the Savior who willingly gave his Life on the cross, and accept Jesus as Lord and Maser of the believer's life from here to eternity.

Once saved, God, in the Person of the Holy Spirit, regenerates a sinner from a hopeless state of sin out of which he or she has no way to climb, into a total eternal security by the acceptance of Jesus as God's Son (Messiah), Lord and Savior. That's God's Great Plan.

All that sounds like a lot of "churchy-speak" for certain. Still, it's important that we remember that salvation is not easy to come by. This world, dominated by sin, does all it can to discourage the acceptance of Jesus as a real Person, much less a total commitment to Him as God in human flesh and Lord and Master of our life. Those not saved are indeed truly lost, as much as they would be in a forest full of trees with no compass and no hope of finding a successful direction. Being lost for eternity is like one who loses his glasses and can't begin to look for them until he finds them. It's just like that. Yet, thank God, holy insight is given to one who asks for it.

Often when we lose hope and think this is the end, God smiles from above and says, "Relax, it's just a bend, it's not the end!"

The Atonement

So why did Jesus die, and why was that the Plan? A simple answer is that Jesus died instead of you and me, a substitutionary death, and in our place, a vicarious death. He "atoned" for our sins.

Walk Saved

He did this when it was you and I who were guilty of death. The righteous God required a payment for our sin. If God didn't, there would be no way we could have any kind of relationship with a sinless Father, while we were in our sin.

In the most profound act of love the world has ever seen, God sent His only Son, Jesus, to redeem the payment for our sin. "Greater love has no one than this," Jesus Himself said, "that he lay down his life for his friends."

That's what Jesus did, for you and me. No one murdered Him. He laid down His Life for His friends. What a supreme privilege it is to call Jesus Christ my friend. But, that's what He is. And we are His.

> *The definition of Love is "meeting needs."*
> W. Oscar Thompson, Jr. (1980)

Awesome!

The word "redemption" comes from the Greek word *agorazo*, which means to purchase something in the marketplace. Jesus redeemed me. He purchased my soul, bought it, just as if my soul was at WalMart and destined for the dumpster unless someone bought it and set it free.

Imagine how it would be if a benevolent buyer bought a man, just so he could free the poor guy from the bondage of a slaves' marketplace. In our case, the price for that freedom was dear. It cost Jesus his own life (I Corinthians 6:20, 7:23 and Revelation 5:9; 14:3-4). Because Jesus died for me, I am His purchased slave, to do His will.

A second Greek word related to our redemption is *exagorazo*, which teaches that Christ redeemed me from the bondage of the law wherein I was condemned. 'Virtually, so I would no longer be subject to the law! First He saved me, then He set me free. Wow!

Finally, the term *lutroo* meaning to obtain release by the payment of a price, applies to the ransom which was paid for me (Luke 24:21), in Christ's blood (I Peter 1:18).

But Jesus' redemption went further than just to pay a price. As God's Son, Jesus fashioned a way that we could be "reconciled" back to God. Think: reconnect the connection. There, on the hill called

Calvary, we were reunited with our loving God, and the enmity and wrath of God on our sin was removed (Romans 5:10).

God always loves the sinner, He just hates the sin.

All this "provisional reconciliation" occurred prior to our faith in God. And even so, we were reconciled to God and rendered savable (II Corinthians 5:18a and 19b).

God said I was savable...

Scholars call the date when one says "Yes" to Jesus as our "experiential reconciliation," when we began to experience that we were actually reconciled to God. On those occasions when God has privileged me to be present when another person makes that decision, I take the opportunity to give the new believer four instructions in beginning their new life. Perhaps this testimony is beyond the study of soteriology per se, but you might like to hear what I tell them:

Instruction One: Tell somebody what you did, and what has happened to you. *"I gave my life to Jesus. I accepted Him as Messiah, Savior and Lord. He came into my life in a brand new way, and the Holy Spirit and my spirit made a solid connection that will never be broken. I am God's child and Jesus is my Lord forever."* It doesn't matter who you tell. You can tell your spouse, your BFF or the waitress at IHOP. In fact, I'd recommend you tell the girl at IHOP. Be excited! This is the greatest thing that can ever happen to you!

Instruction Two: Open your eyes and look up. Look for God's confirmation. God has never failed to confirm His agreement with the new believer. Look for it. And, when it happens, don't chalk it up to something strange or extraordinary, to luck, to good fortune, or to anything but what it is - a work of God. God will manifest His pleasure in accepting you into the Lamb's Book of Life and in reserving your place in His Heaven. I'll guarantee that God's confirmation will be exciting, too. It'll most certainly put a smile on your face and a bounce in your step!

Instruction Three: Get a good Bible, if you don't already own one. I like the King James Version, because I love the poetic sound. And, as I've told many others, "If it was good enough for Paul and Silas, it's good enough for me," which is a silly statement at best. Truth is, in my study

I also use the New International Version, New American Standard Version and even the Good News Bible (Today's English Version). All these versions have a goal of being are accurate and identical, except in the phraseology. So find the one you like and enjoy, then read it.

Instruction Four: Read the Gospel of John, cover to cover. If you set aside the uninterrupted time, you can do it in an hour or two. OK, maybe a little more. It's only 21 chapters. It's very basic, and you'll soon have a deeper understanding of the love and purpose of God, Jesus and the Holy Spirit than you've ever had before. You might enjoy it so much you'll want to read it twice!

God's purpose for you is to be like Jesus (Ephesians 4:11-24).

Jesus' purpose for you is to have joy (John 15:11). He said, *"These things have I spoken unto you, that my joy might remain in you, and that your joy might be full."*

In His death, Jesus became our "propitiation," in fully satisfying all the righteous demands of God toward us, the sinner. Jesus covered our sin. God provided the remedy. God provided the gift, of His own son, Jesus for us (John 3:16), as if we were the only person on Earth.

God both legally and graciously forgave us of all charges that were held against us by our sin. God cancelled our debt. Wiped it out. Tore it up. Our sins were banished as far as the East is from the West. They are no more. All our sins are gone, gone, gone: past, present and future. This forgiveness is distinct from the daily cleansing we need to maintain our fellowship with God. That comes as a result of our prayer and confession as a born-again Christian.

> *...as if I was the only person on Earth!*

That's why many say that a Christian's life needs to be "prayer-conditioned!" A lot of kneeling will keep a person in good standing. Besides, it's hard to stumble when you're down on your knees. I have a friend in God, He calls me Friend!

Since Jesus paid the price, God declares us "justified," just-as-if we had never sinned. We are pardoned and our sins are removed. We are looked upon by God as righteous, with the same righteousness of Jesus

Christ. Once His, we are welcome into Heaven. All this is done for us apart from any good works we may perform (Romans 4:5). It is done through our faith (Romans 5:9), and our trust in Him.

What is faith? Well, it is certainly a sidebar to soteriology. A good acronym for faith is F. A. I. T. H., meaning Forsaking All, I Trust Him. Think about that every time you find a coin on the ground. What does it say on the coin? *"In God We Trust."* Wow, look at that! God drops a message right in front of you reminding you to trust Him! How can any God-follower pass it by?

So, pick up that coin and let it help develop your faith. How do you build a strong faith? Here it is: Faith is directly proportional to the number of times one can recall God acting in his or her life.

Will everyone be saved? The simple and sad answer is no. It's a limited atonement, and here's why:

Limited Atonement

Christ died for everyone, but not everyone will be saved. The atonement of Christ is limited to a definite and particular group of people. Yes, Jesus laid down His life for His sheep (John 10:15), but not everyone is included in the flock. Since the objects of the Father's love are particular, definite and limited, so are the objects of Christ's death.[1]

When the Bible talks of all being saved, it is referring to all classes of people but not every person (II Corinthians 5:15). Still, make no mistake: ALL are surely invited. It is the Father's wish that ALL be saved. God tells us in Revelation 22:17, *"And whosoever will, let him take the water of life freely."*

There's more, read on.

Unlimited Atonement

Evangelicals believe that atonement is unlimited, that is, that Christ died for every person, and that's true, but His death is effective only to those who believe the gospel. Taken at face value, the statements of the New Testament teach that Christ died for everyone. The world, as John describes it, is God-hating, Christ-rejecting and Satan-dominated. Yet, it is for the world that Christ died.[2] But, if Christ died for everyone and everyone is not saved, then God's Plan is thwarted. Unlimited atonement simply means the atonement is *available* to everyone. What is limited is not the atonement, but the *reception* of it. Only believers in the gospel will be atoned for.

The Process of Salvation: the Work of the Father

So then, is there a doctrine of "election" and does the Bible teach that kind of salvation? There are some indicators in the Bible:

Israel is elect (Deuteronomy 7:6),
angels are elect (I Timothy 5:21),
the Levitical Priests were elect (Deuteronomy 18:5), even
Jeremiah the prophet was elect (Jeremiah 1:5).

And, in Ephesians 1:4, Paul says that *"He chose us."* In that, certain people were called out from the masses, if the theology of election be true.

"Predestination," from the Greek word *proorizo,* occurs six times in the New Testament, meaning to mark out beforehand. Predestination says that God by His sovereign choice marked out certain believers in eternity past.

OK, let's clear it up. The qualifier is this: Election and predestination don't, however, take away a person's responsibility. There it is. Even though election and predestination are clearly taught in Scripture, a person is still held accountable for his choices. Scripture never suggests that a person is lost because he's not elect or had not been predestined. No, Scripture says a person is lost because he refuses to believe. A person is lost because he refuses to believe. It's worth it to say it twice.

> *Election and predestination don't, however, take away a person's responsibility. There it is.*

To be saved we must believe.

In our adoption, we are placed in a new position as that of a son or daughter and given all the natural-born rights of a fully-legitimate son in God's family. We become an heir to God's estate. Our old life is completely wiped out, all debts are cancelled. We are released from slavery into the freedom and maturity in Christ (Romans 8:15 and Galatians 4:6). Paul, in Ephesians, connects our adoption with predestination which took place in eternity past, but - don't be confused - our adoption wasn't realized until we believed in Jesus. That is, until we made the decision to accept God's Gift of full and free salvation. John 1:12 says, *"To all who believed in Him [Jesus] and accepted him, he gave the right to become children of God. They are reborn - not with a physical birth resulting from human passion or plan, but a birth that comes from God"* (New Living Translation).

> *Scripture never suggests that a person is lost because he's not elect or had not been predestined. No, Scripture says a person is lost because he refuses to believe.*

Election, predestination and adoption are all the work of the Father. We are adopted.

The Process of Salvation: the Work of the Son

When we accept Jesus, our sin debt is paid and we secure a release from our penalty and bondage of sin. The righteous demand of our holy God is met. But, more than that, we are set apart or "sanctified."

Sanctification is like the chair we pull out when the guys get together for a football game on Harry's big-screen TV. Or, when the ladies gather at a Tupperware party. As we enter the room, we pick out a resting place, a chair, and sanctify it. Sounds strange, doesn't it? Well, think about it. We're setting that chair apart for a specific purpose of holding our body for an hour or so. (Yeah, some might say "Poor chair.") Sanctification in Christ is much the same. When He saved us, He set us apart, to be holy and for His purpose.

In our "positional sanctification," we are accounted holy before God, declared a saint, through the once-and-for-all death of our Savior (Hebrews 10:10, 14, 29). How cool is that?

Our "experiential sanctification" takes place in our daily life (I Thessalonians 5:23), and it grows as we mature in our walk (Romans 6:12 and 12:1-2), nourished by the wonderful Word of God (Psalms 199:9-16). How wonderful it is to be in God's care!

Our "ultimate sanctification" will be in the future, when we're transformed into the likeness of Christ, and when Jesus will present us before God as unblemished (Ephesians 5:26-27). Paul himself wrassled with this. He said, *"For to me to live is Christ, and to die is gain"* (Philippians 1:21). His meaning is, there'd be an advantage in dying and experiencing eternal life, above that of living here. The only reason why he should wish at all to live here was, that he might be the means of benefitting others. In Philippians 1:24-25, Paul explains what's in it for a Christian to actually look forward to dying:

> In dying, the Christian will be freed from sin. In Heaven he will sin no more, one of the reasons it's "Heaven."
>
> In dying, the Christian will be freed from doubts about his condition. While we're here, the best of us can't help but have doubts about our personal walk. Is it good enough? The more "mature (Bible word)" a Christian becomes, the more he or she realizes that our security is sure. After all, our salvation wasn't perpetuated by us. In fact, we had nothing to do with it, but to accept it. It was and is all Jesus. So, yes, once saved, always saved. Jesus makes no mistakes. See "God's confirmation" above.
>
> In dying, the Christian will be freed from temptation. Won't that be a major blessing? Here on Earth, no one knows when he or she may be tempted, nor how powerful the temptation may be. The Bible warns us to *"be sober, be vigilant; because your adversary the devil, as a roaring lion, walks about, seeking whom he may devour"* (I Peter 5:8).
>
> Are we saved from Satan's would-be attacks? Yes.
>
> Will he still try to tempt us. Certainly.

But, in Heaven, there'll be no allurement to lead a Christian astray. There will be no artful, cunning, and skillful schemes of Satan to induce us to sin. Even here, Satan has no dominion over the Christian. He knows he has no remedy for the Blood, which covers it all, and the Grace and Mercy of God, which forgives any and all transgressions. Forget temptations. While they may come, they can't succeed. Like we say in the Army, "Hoo-rah!"

> *Satan knows he has no remedy for the Blood, which covers it all, and the Grace and Mercy of God, which forgives it all!*

In dying, the Christian will be delivered from all his enemies - from the slanderer, the accuser, the persecutor. While here, the Christian constantly hears that tired old phrase, *"...And you call yourself a Christian?"* (mostly from unbelievers) with each transgression or apparent transgression. Especially by the lost, our motives are called in question, and sometimes they are even met with detraction and slander, right? Well, in Heaven, there'll be no such accusations to do the Christian injustice. More important, in Heaven, every soul there will rejoice in knowing that he or she is pure, saved, bought and paid for by the Blood of Jesus. Wow!

In dying, the Christian will be delivered from suffering. No more pain. No more sickness. No more sadness. No more suffering. No more separations. No more relationship problems. No more financial problems. No more doubt. No more questions. No more tears. Jesus' joy in John 15:11 is real, constant and ever-present. Heaven is, well, heavenly.

We're saved *from*, and we're saved *to*.

Thank you, Jesus!

The Process of Salvation: the Work of the Spirit

It's the Spirit's job to convict the sinner, to regenerate the believer into a new life, to indwell the believer and baptize him into union with Christ and other Christians. The Holy Spirit seals the believer in an everlasting relationship with God (Ephesians 4:30).

Once sealed, always sealed!

The Process of Salvation: the Work of the Believer

Scriptures tell us that our only responsibility in salvation is to believe in Christ and the gospel, as in John 1:12; 3:16, 18, 36; 5:24; 11:25-26; 12:44; 20:31; Acts 16:31 and I John 5:13, to name a few. That's true, yet let's understand what salvation is not:

To repent and believe will not earn a sinner salvation. One must change one's mind about sin and trust Christ alone for salvation. The Bible says the devils believe and tremble in terror (James 2:19). They sure aren't saved. No, this kind of belief is simply *intellectual* belief. Saving belief is a *trusting* belief. It's not just faith that the chair will support you, it's placing your weight in the chair!

To believe and be baptized will not earn a sinner salvation. One is baptized as a demonstration of a profession of faith in Christ. You can be baptized in every mudhole between here and Tuscaloosa, Alabama, 'til all the tadpoles know you by name. That won't get you saved!

To confess Christ will not earn a sinner salvation. One must acknowledge His deity, confess and believe. Paul tells us that if you confess with your mouth that Jesus is Lord (commit to Him as Master of everything you do) and believe in your heart that God raised him from the dead (accept Him as your Savior), you will be saved. You've got to believe!

To exercise blind faith will not earn a sinner salvation. One must seek salvation with knowledge, conviction and trust. How many of us came down the aisle as a little kid and didn't have a clue as to what we were doing? The whole Daily Vacation Bible School class was doing it, and we sure didn't want to be left out, right? Besides, it was fun having all those old folks make a fuss over us. That won't get you saved. Sorry, Gramma.

Saving faith involves knowledge, the intellect to believe certain basic truths for salvation. It's not all automatic, as some evangelists would preach. Salvation requires a certain amount of understanding. A believer must think, at least enough to understand basic truths. This is why one must be very careful with small kids who want to be baptized.

To be saved:

One must be sorry for, and repent of his or her sins;

One must believe in God and believe that Jesus is God (Romans 10:9-10);

One must believe that Jesus is all He claimed to be, otherwise one would die in his sins (John 8:24);

One must believe in basic truths: Man's sinfulness, Christ's atoning sacrifice and Jesus' bodily resurrection;

One must believe in faith that Jesus is the Son of God; and,

One must believe in the heart that God raised Him from the dead; and,

One must be willing to confess with the mouth all the above.

Works can't save you either. Only faith in Jesus can save you. It's not that works can save you, it's that once saved, works are a natural by-product of the joy of being saved.

Works can't save you!

James says faith without works is dead (James 2:17).

The Jewish Torah (first five Books of the Bible) and in particular Deuteronomy, makes it real clear. Once saved, a believer takes on a totally new attitude. So the *Shema*, as the Jews call it, becomes a natural thing to do as Moses tells it in Deuteronomy 6:5: *"Thou shalt love the LORD thy God with all thine heart, and with all thy soul, and with all thy might."*

Ask any born-again believer, and he'll tell you, *"Yeah, I do that. Not because it's a commandment, as Jesus instructed it, but because I love Jesus, and He is everything to me. I love to love Him that way!"*

True conviction, the kind that opens the door to salvation, is wrought with emotion, but that emotion and that conviction testifies of truthfulness.

Trust is key, knowing that Jesus will fulfill His part of the equation. He always does, and that's forever. It's not about us. It's all about Jesus.

Before U were thought of or time had begun,
God stuck U in the name of His Son.
And each time U pray, you'll see it's true,
You can't spell out JesUs and not include U.
> You're a pretty big part of His wonderful name,
> For U, He was born; that's why He came.
> And His great love for U is the reason He died.
> It even takes U to spell crUcified.

Isn't it thrilling and splendidly grand
He rose from the dead, with U in His plan?
The stones split away, the gold trUmpet blew,
and this word resUrrection is spelled with a U.
> When JesUs left Earth at His upward ascension,
> He felt there was one thing He just had to mention.
> 'Go into the world and tell them it's true
> That I love them all - Just like I love U.'

So many great people are spelled with a U,
Don't they have a right to know JesUs too?
It all depends now on what U will do,
He'd like them to know,
But it all starts with U.

Jesus added to the Shema command to *"Love your neighbor as yourself"* in His teaching of the greatest commandment (Luke 10:27). It surely takes work, action if you will, to do that!

Grace

No study of soteriology, salvation, is complete without an understanding of grace. What a wonderful word, what a wonderful concept. Grace is the unmerited favor of God toward all men displayed in His general care of them.[3] As preachers like to say, God gives rain to the atheistic farmer just the same as He does to the saved one.

Grace is particularly exhibited when God withholds judgment to the sinner, so that person can repent instead (Romans 2:4). *"You don't deserve this,"* God could say, *"but I'm just going give it to you anyway. Just because I love you."* If that doesn't humble you, then, wow, what will?

God's grace restrains sin.

> Although Laban cheated Jacob, God restrained the deceit of Laban (Genesis 31:7).
>
> When Satan challenged God concerning Job's loyalty to Him, God restrained what Satan could do to him (Job 1:12, 2:6).
>
> God restrains through the work of the Holy Spirit and through the prophets, Whose work is to bring man to repentance, not to condemn him.
>
> Even today, there's a restraint by the Holy Spirit, noted in I Thessalonians 2:6-7, who holds back the forces of Satan, who will be released one day in the future. Pentecostalists claim this vociferously.

God's grace convicts the whole world of sin. John 16:8-11 tells us that *"God will convict the world of sin and judgment."* Even so, only some will come.

If you don't like the way you were born, try being born again.

God's Grace is the only reason we can be saved. The Bible tells us, *"For it is by grace you have been saved, through faith - and this not from yourselves, it is the gift of God - not by works, so that no one can boast"* (Ephesians 2: 8-9).

Clearly before one can be born-again, there must be
> a conviction,
> a witness from God and thereby
> a knowledge of God.

Everyone knows about God, but the Holy Spirit convicts persons of the real-ness of their sins and the righteousness of Jesus who saves. There's a difference, and it's a life-changer when we're talking about soteriology.

What scholars call "efficacious grace" is the work of the Holy Spirit which effectively moves men to believe in Jesus as Savior.[4] When people become willing to believe in Jesus, they are empowered by the Holy Spirit and accorded efficacious grace. Efficacious grace is limited to the elect, who become elect because they recognize that they are called and chosen as a result of their desire for Jesus in their lives. Efficacious grace is never successfully rejected once God moves upon a sinner's desire and will, but won't move contrary to a person's will. The grace is there, but one must accept it. We do have a role in salvation. It's when we say, "I Have Decided To Follow Jesus."

Jesus tells us another example of efficacious grace in John 6:44, *"No man cometh unto Me unless the Father who sent Me draws him."* That drawing power of God leads to the conviction of a person's sin. Once we're convicted of sin, we can understand and receive God's grace. This is something like the power of prayer for an unsaved loved one.

When we were singing as *"Buddy Merrick & Praise,"* we used to say during our concerts, *"If you're unsaved and someone is praying you into the Kingdom, you might as well come on down now, because God and they won't let up!"*

It was always amazing how folks would tell us afterward, *"I could feel those prayers that people were praying for me. They just kept, like, illuminating my mind!"*

Regeneration

Once a person accepts God's offer of salvation, another blessed event occurs: "regeneration," or the communication of divine life to the soul. God imparts a new nature, or heart, and actually produces a new creation. New! The Bible says, *"Therefore, if any man be in Christ, he is a new creature; old things are passed away; behold, all things are become new"* (II Corinthians 5:17). What a wonderful promise. We are re-generated, brought back to the innocence of Adam, just as if we'd never sinned at all. Awesome!

It's a wonderful experience, too, for the Christian. Once born-again and saved, every Christian will attest to a new life. Christ's Words echoes Paul's Scripture, when he tells us, *"Verily, verily, I say unto thee, Except a man be born again, he cannot see the Kingdom of God"* (John 3:3).

Christians wonder sometimes why an unbeliever can't see the logic of seeking the saving grace of Jesus and a rebirth into the new dimension of this new spiritual life. Well, here's the answer: to seek spiritual things with natural eyes is a virtual impossibility in an earthly sense. The things of God are not of this world, they are of heaven and of spirit. The unsaved can't possibly "see" the things of God. Only the spirit within a born-again believer can "know" the Holy Spirit of God, and with it, all those *things* which Jesus said would bring us a fulfilling *joy,* just like His. One must have "Spiritual eyes" to see Jesus.

One Christmas we were singing in the choir a special musical program for our Texas Baptist church. On the last song, *"Glory To Your Name,"* we got overwhelmingly deluged by the Holy Spirit of God. Man, we were singing! Not just with our voices, but, no kidding, with our whole hearts! By the last note, even men were shaking, wiping tears, including me. I remember years back when Fred Johnson was singing, *"Pass Me Not"* on Jimmy Swaggart's TV Show and lost it. He said to Jimmy Swaggart right on-air, *"Man, Brudder Jimmy, somet'in' done got in dat song..."* I know what he meant. The old Buddy would never have experienced that. That's regeneration!

For sure, regeneration is something done *upon* a person, not *by* him. We can't bring about regeneration no matter how many Wednesday nights we devote to it, or how many pews we jump at invitation time. Regeneration is the work of the Holy Spirit.

Earthly birth is a product of one's parents. Spiritual birth is a creation of God.

Our earthly birth was begot by a corruptible seed, but our Spiritual birth is incorruptible.

In our earthly birth, we were made a slave of Satan by our original sin (painful but true), but when we were born again, we became Christ's free man.

Once, we were an object of divine wrath (ow!), but now we are an object of divine love (ahh!).

That's regeneration!

Once Saved, Always Saved

The Arminian theologians teach that a person has received his salvation as an act of his will and he may forfeit his salvation as an act of the will, or through specific sins.

The Calvinist says that the true believer will persevere in his faith, the so-called "perseverance of the saints (the "P" in the acronym TULIP)."[5]

The truth is, all believers will backslide. I love Jesus with all my heart, but I know I have sinned and backslidden more than many. Yet, I also realize that it wasn't me who saved me, it was my Lord, Jesus, and the blood He shed for me. I can fail. He can't. Can't. Because I genuinely believe, and believed then in Christ as my Savior. I am forever secured by God and His keeping power (not mine). The blood will never lose its power.

The extraordinary thing is that, as I mature in my faith and belief, continued by diligent study of various doctrines and beliefs, I become more aware and more firm in my belief that Jesus saved me once and for all.

Jesus never fails.

Hallelujah!

We are saved because of the securing work of the Father (Romans 8:28-30). Jesus tells the Father in John 17:12, that none are lost who are His, and that includes all believers.

We are saved because of the securing work of the Son. Jesus has
> redeemed us (Ephesians 1:7),
> removed the wrath of God from us (Romans 3:25),
> justified us (Romans 5:1),
> forgiven us (Colossians 2:13) and
> sanctified us to a special place with Him (John 17:24).

Jesus still
> prays for me,
> intercedes for me and
> patiently awaits for the day when I will be with Him (John 17:24).

Therefore, we can comfortably reject any view that says we can lose our salvation. If we could lose our salvation, then Jesus would be ineffective in all His securing work as our Mediator. And, that's just not true.

We are saved because of the securing work of the Holy Spirit. He has regenerated us into a new creature, in love with God, with new life and the Holy Spirit indwelt in us. We are sealed in our salvation for the day of redemption (Ephesians 4:30). Sealed! Our future inheritance is guaranteed by the Holy Spirit.

Summary

Paul asks two crucial questions in Romans 8:33-34,
> *"Who will bring a charge against God's elect? God is the one who justifies.*
>
> *Who is the one that condemns? Christ Jesus is He who died, yes, rather who was raised, who is at the right hand of God, who intercedes for us."*

No one can condemn us, because Christ is our advocate.

Romans 8:30 declares,
> *"And those He predestined, He also called;*
> *those He called, He also justified;*
> *those He justified, He also glorified."*

This verse tells me that from the moment God invited me to accept Jesus, it was as if I was "glorified" in His presence in Heaven, like, right now. Once "justified," my salvation is guaranteed. I'm just as secure as if I was already in Heaven. Paul knew that. So do I.

Now born-again, I've been "regenerated," and for me to become un-saved, well, I'd have to be un-regenerated, which would un-do the work of God the Father, God the Son and God the Holy Ghost. Do you believe the Word? Then rest in the fact that the Bible gives no evidence that our new birth can be taken away.

Take a tea bag and put it into a glass of water. What happens? The tea immediately affects the very essence of the water, its "wateriness" so to speak. And, the water wonderfully changes into a great, tasty drink. Can the drink ever lose its tea-ness? No! How do you take the tea out of the water? You can't. Once tea'd, always tea'd.

The Scripture says it best itself, *"For I am convinced that neither death nor life, neither angels nor demons, neither the present nor the future, nor any powers, neither height nor depth, nor anything else in all creation, will be able to separate us* [me] *from the love of God that is in Christ Jesus our Lord"* (Romans 8:38-39). The same God who saved us is the same God who will keep us, as Jesus prayed in the Garden of Gethsemane (see John 17:11).

Once tea'd, always tea'd!

John 3:15 states that whoever believes in Jesus Christ will have eternal life. In our salvation, we are saved, regenerated, justified, sanctified and glorified, and that's forever.

We are saved by faith, not of works (Ephesians 2:8), yet our heart yearns to work good works, for that's what we're created to do (Ephesians 2:10). Better yet, God prepares those good works even before we set out to do them.

I don't boast of my salvation, but I do delight to walk in it. Hey, I'm saved!

> *Saved to the uttermost, I am the Lord's;*
> *Jesus my Savior salvation affords;*
> *Gives me His Spirit a witness within,*
> *Whisp'ring of pardon, and saving from sin.*
> *Saved, saved, saved to the uttermost:*
> *Saved, saved by power divine;*
> *Saved, saved, I'm saved to the uttermost;*
> *Jesus the Savior is mine!*[6]

Hebrews 7:25 says, "He is able also to save them to the uttermost that come unto God by Him." And, thank God, He saved me.

So what do we do now? Tell them! Here's how Gloria Gaither's going to do it:

> *"I'm gonna sing just as long as it takes for a song to make sad, heavy spirits free;*

> *I'm gonna keep making music that carries the secret that Jesus is liberty;*
>
> *I'm gonna turn off the sounds that would drag people down to the pit of despondency;*
>
> *With the sweet happy tune He is coming soon for His children like you and me!"*[7]

---

[1] Palmer, Edwin H., *The Five Points of Calvinism* (Grand Rapids: Guardian, 1972), pg. 44.

[2] Elwell, Walter A., *Evangelical Dictionary of Theology* (Grand Rapids: Baker, 1984), pg. 594.

[3] Ryrie, Charles C., *The Holy Spirit* (Chicago: Moody, 1965), pg. 55. Ryrie's *The Grace of God* (Chicago, Moody, 1963) offers a more broad discussion of grace.

[4] Berkof, Louis, *Systematic Theology* (Grand Rapids: Eerdmans, 1941), pg. 436.

[5] John Calvin (1509–1564) was an influential French theologian and pastor during the Protestant Reformation. His system of Christian theology called Calvinism included five major components, using the acronym TULIP:
  *T*otal depravity,
  *U*nconditional election,
  *L*imited atonement,
  *I*rresistible grace and
  *P*erseverance of the saints.

In Calvin's theology: Total depravity means that sin is in every part of one's being, including the mind and will, so that a man cannot save himself. In unconditional election, God chooses to save people unconditionally; that is, they are not chosen on the basis of their own merit. Limited atonement means the sacrifice of Christ on the cross was for the purpose of saving the elect. Irresistible grace means that when God has chosen to save someone, He will. Perseverance of the saints means that those people God chooses cannot lose their salvation; they will continue to believe. If they fall away, it will be only for a time.

[6] *"Saved to the Uttermost"* was written and composed by William James Kirkpatrick (1838-1921). Kirkpatrick is best known as a composer of tunes for Fanny Crosby's *"He Hideth My Soul"* and *"Redeemed, How I Love to Proclaim It,"* Priscilla Owens's *"Jesus Saves"* and Louisa Stead's *"'Tis So Sweet to Trust in Jesus,"* among others. *"Saved To The Uttermost"* was copyrighted in 1889 and may have been first published in

the 1890 collection, *The Finest of the Wheat*, edited by George Elderkin and published by R. R. McCabe of Chicago, IL.

[7] *"I'm Gonna Sing"* by Gloria Gaither, is sung on the album, *"Everything Good,"* by the wonderful Gaither Vocal Band, with Guy Penrod in the lead, Russ Taff, David Phelps and Bill Gaither. I can't believe on the You Tube video, no one stood! Are you kidding me? I would have been ready for the rapture! Wow!

V. Walk with Jesus

Christology - Is He was, or is He is?

Preface

"No Jesus - no peace, know Jesus, know peace." Good advice.
Christology is a study of the doctrine of Christ.
In Christ alone my hope is found; He is my light, my strength, my song.[1]

Let's begin this chapter with a profound understatement, and that is this:

No man, in the history of man, has impacted man like Jesus Christ.

Face to face, Christ taught only a relative handful of people here on Earth, yet His teachings have transformed the world.

He has been written in more poems and songs, depicted in more paintings, sculptures and works than any artist in history.

> *No man, in the history of man, has impacted man, like Jesus Christ.*

His life and work can't be denied. For Him to impact us as He has, is no less an amazing feat.

Jesus had no servants, yet many still call Him Master.

He had no degree, yet He's still the world's greatest Teacher.

Had no medicines, yet every day multitudes still call Him Healer.

He had no army, yet kings and rulers still fear Him.

He won no military battles, yet He conquered the world.
He committed no crime, yet they crucified Him.
He was buried in a tomb, yet He lives today.
Elders could not explain Him.
Waves could not wash over Him.
Time could not limit Him.
Satan could not defeat Him.
Herod could not destroy Him.
The grave could not hold Him.
He's One of a Kind.

Jesus is... in every book of the Bible.

He is God.
He's the Son of God.
Jesus is the Second Person of the Trinity, equal with God yet submissive in office. What Theology Proper says about God, it maintains about Jesus. Since God is eternal, so is Christ.

He is the King of kings and the Lord of lords.
I asked my Father one day, "Who was Jesus?"
My Father said, "My son, Jesus isn't *gone*, Jesus *Is*."
In Genesis, *Jesus Is...* the Creator.
> *He's* the True Beginning and the Infallible Word.
> *Jesus Is...* the Seed of the Woman.
> *He's* Able's Lamb,
> *He's* Noah's Ark,
> *He's* Abraham's Ram, Isaac's Well, Jacob's Ladder and Joseph's Dream.

In Exodus, *Jesus Is...* the Lamb and the Blood of the Passover.
In Leviticus, the Tabernacle and the Priesthood.
In Numbers, *He's* God's Provision in a Cloud by day and a Pillar of Fire by night.
And in Deuteronomy, *Jesus Is...* a Great Prophet, like Moses, Who will lead His people to a promised land.
In Joshua, *He's* the Scarlet Thread, that Tie that binds our hearts in Christian love.

Walk with Jesus

In Judges, *He's* the Jawbone of the ass.
In Ruth, the Redeemer of the kinsmen.
And, in I & II Samuel *Jesus Is...* the Sweet Singer of Israel.
In I & II Kings, *He's* The Temple and The Holy of Holies.
In I & II Chronicles *and* Ezra, *He's* The Restoration of the backslider, and in Nehemiah *and* Esther, *He's* The Victory for the Christian.
Oh, in Job, we know of *Jesus* as Patience and Trust, and, in Psalms, the Poet, the Shepherd, and the Great Choir.
In Proverbs, *He's* Wisdom,
    and in Ecclesiastes, *He's* the Teacher of that wisdom.
    and, in Song of Solomon, *He's* the Rose of Sharon and the Lily of the Valley.
In Isaiah, *He's* a Wonderful and Mighty God, the Prince of Peace, and yet, the Suffering Savior.
In Jeremiah, *He's* the Balm of Gilead.
In Lamentations, the Weeping Prophet.
    Still, in Ezekiel, *He's* the Wheel in the middle of the wheel.
In Daniel, the Fourth Man in the furnace.
In Hosea, *He is* the Regatherer of Israel,
    and, in Joel, *Jesus Is...* the Poured-out Baptism in the Holy Spirit.
In Amos, *He's* the Eternal Kingdom.
In Obadiah, the Deliverer.
In Jonah, *He's* the God of Second Chances.
In Micah, the Millennia.
In Nahum, Habakkuk *and* Zephaniah, the Day of the Lord.
In Haggai *and* Zechariah, *He's* our Coming Revival.
    And in Malachi, *Jesus Is...* our Precious Savior, rising with healing in His wings.
In Matthew, *He's* the King.
In Mark, *He's* the Savior.
In Luke, *He's* Man.
In John, *He's* God.
In The Acts, *He's* the Holy Spirit.

In Romans, *He's* Grace.

In I & II Corinthians, *He's* the Gifts of the Spirit.

In Galatians, Ephesians, Philippians and Colossians. He's our New Covenant, and in I & II Thessalonians, our Blessed Hope.

We see the *Person of Jesus* in I & II Timothy as the Preacher and the Deacon.

In Titus *and* Philemon, *He's* our Pastor.

In Hebrews, our Great High Priest.

In James, our Great Healer.

In I & II Peter, *He's* Precious Blood.

In I, II & III John, *He's* Perfect Love.

And in the Book of Jude, *Jesus Is...* the Original Faith and that Old Time Religion.

And, in The Revelation, *Jesus Is...* the Lamb that taketh away the sins of the world,

He's the Vision,

He's the Churches,

He's the 7-Sealed Book,

He's the 7 Trumpets,

He's the 7 Seals,

He's the 7 Vials,

He's the 2 Witnesses,

He's the Woman Clothed with the Sun,

He is... the New Jerusalem,

Jesus Is... the King of Kings and the Lord of Lords,

Jesus Is... the Fairest of Ten Thousand,

Jesus Is... Jehovah, Lord, God Almighty, the Maker of Heaven and of Earth,

Jesus Is... God, in Three Persons: God, the Father, God, the Son, and God, the Holy Ghost,

Jesus Is... The Alpha and Omega, the Beginning and the End,

Jesus is, Jesus was, and Jesus evermore shall be the Messiah, the Redeemer,

He is... Jesus Christ, The King of Glory![3]

The Son of God was born into this world through a human birth to a virgin, yet He existed from eternity past. He is not limited by time. He has no beginning and will have no end. His preexistence and the proofs of His eternality likewise document the proof of His deity with God and *vice versa*.

Jesus is God.

There are 93 Names of Jesus above, but in reality, there are hundreds of Names of Jesus that could have been included there. Christology encompasses many concepts as well, including the prophesies of Jesus Christ as published in both the Old and New Testaments,
>
> the human side of Jesus, and
> the Person of His deity,
> His hypostatic union (Jesus is both human and divine)
> His life's work on Earth,
> His present day ministry and
> His glorious Second Coming.

Jesus Is... Prophesy in the Old Testament, Fulfilment in the New

Micah 5:2 tells us that Jesus, the product of Bethlehem, has been with us from eternity. In Isaiah 9:6, Jesus is called the *"Eternal Father."*

The Person of Christ was foreshadowed by a dozen men of the Old Testament, including:
>
> Adam, the first born;
> Noah, called a Second Adam;
> Abraham, the father of the faith;
> Melchizadek, the king of righteousness;
> Joseph, abused, betrayed and exalted;
> Moses, the deliverer of the law;
> Joshua, who led God's people into the Promised Land;
> Samuel, the prophet who was favored by God;
> David, the man after God's own heart;
> Elijah and Elisha, who called God's people to repent;
> and Zerubbabel and Joshua, who rebuilt the temple,

All were accused by Satan and all were defended by God.

Jesus Himself was not only prophesied, but He fulfilled all those many prophesies:

> Jesus in Genesis 3:15 is known as the *proevangelium*, the first prophesy of Christ. The Scripture references "her seed" and points to the virgin birth.
>
> Jesus fulfils the Abrahamic Covenant in Genesis 12 as interpreted by both Matthew (Matthew 1:1) and Paul (Galatians 3:16) in the New Testament.
>
> Jesus came from the line of Issac and again is the fulfillment of God's Covenant with Isaac (Genesis 17:19).
>
> Jesus came from the line of Judah and is affirmed as the Messiah King in Genesis 49:10.
>
> Jesus came from the line of David as prophesied in II Samuel 7:12-16 and Psalms 89, to rule eternally.

"This gift of love and righteousness, Scorned by the ones He came to save."[1]

Jesus' lineage, His virgin birth, His life's mission, ministry, teaching, presentation and rejection, His death and resurrection, His victory and ascension and His everlasting reign as sovereign King are all prophesied in the Old Testament and fulfilled in the New Testament.

"Jesus possessed neither wealth nor influence. His relatives were inconspicuous, and had neither training nor formal education. In infancy, He startled a king; in childhood, He puzzled doctors; in manhood, He ruled the course of nature, walked upon the billows as if pavement and hushed the sea to sleep. He healed the multitudes without medicine and made no charge for His service. The names of the past proud statesmen of Greece and Rome have come and gone. The names of the past scientists, philosophers and theologians have come and gone; but the Name of this Man abounds more and more. Though time has spread nineteen hundred years between the people of this generation and the scene of His crucifixion, yet He lives."

"The Incomparable Christ" by J. Oswald Sanders[2]

Augustine said, *"The New Testament is in the Old concealed; the Old Testament is in the New revealed."* Surely Jesus Is... in the New Testament as well as the Old, he was prophesied to appear, fulfilled prophesies on Earth and still does in the Person of the Holy Spirit.

"In Christ alone, who took on flesh, Fullness of God in helpless babe."[1]

Isaiah 7:14 promised a sign to the unbelieving King Ahaz, that a virgin would bear a son who would be called Immanuel, which means "God with us."

Micah 5:2 identifies the birthplace of Jesus as Bethlehem, though it be little among the towns of Judah.

In Isaiah 40:3, we find John the Baptist, the forerunner, who would prepare the way for Jesus (Malachi 3:1 and Matthew 3:3).

The virgin birth was the means whereby the incarnation of Christ took place, whereby the eternal Son of God took to Himself an additional nature, that is, humanity. Christ remains forever unblemished deity which He has had from eternity past; but He also possesses true, sinless humanity in one person forever (John 1:14, Philippians 2:7-8 and I Timothy 3:16).[5]

The virgin birth is no mystery to a believer. Matthew and Luke are very clear in their publishing of the wonderful narrative. Matthew 1:18 emphasizes that Mary was pregnant before she and Joseph lived together or had any intimate relationship, and the Bible goes on to explain (verses 22-23) that the Holy Spirit induced her condition. She remained a virgin until Jesus was born.

Prophesied and Fulfilled: The Life of Jesus

"This cornerstone, this solid ground, Firm through the fiercest drought and storm[1]*."*

Christ's mission on Earth was clear and was well-prophesied. Isaiah 61:1 promises that the Holy Spirit would anoint Jesus for His ministry, empower Him to preach to the poor, and give sight to the blind (Luke 4:18-19). The Old Testament in Isaiah 1:9 predicts that Jesus would be identified with the despised of society and with the Gentiles. That prediction, too, came true.

Jesus came from Heaven (John 3:13) in His deity. Mary's pregnancy was simply the means of His becoming human flesh (John 1:1).

Jesus created all things (John 1:3).

Jesus is *Adonai* (Lord God, King of kings) in Matthew 22:44.

Jesus is the Second Person of the Trinity. Jesus is the One of the Three who is called *Lord,* or *Yahweh,* in the incident recorded in Genesis 18, thus the Second Person of the Trinity.[4] The identification of Christ with the appearances of the Angel of the Lord, the theophany, can be demonstrated in the fact that the Angel of the Lord no longer appears after the incarnation of Christ and the Angel of the Lord does not appear anywhere in the New Testament. That's interesting, isn't it?

Of Christ's ministry, Isaiah's prophesy in Isaiah 53:4 of the Old Testament foretells that Jesus would bear the sickness of the people, which Matthew 8:17 affirms in the New Testament as becoming true.

Isaiah 35:5-6 and 61:1-2 describes Jesus' earthly ministries of restoring sight to the blind, healing the lame, cleansing the lepers, raising the dead and preaching the good news to the poor. All these things He did, as recorded in the New Testament.

Even Psalms 78:2 foretold that Christ would teach in parables and how wonderful they are! In History, Jesus came to preach the Gospel. In Eternity He came so there would be a Gospel to preach!

In History, Jesus came to preach the Gospel.
In Eternity, Jesus came so there would be a Gospel to preach!

Zechariah 9:9 describes the triumphal entry of Christ, praised as the king of Jerusalem riding an unbroken donkey (Matthew 21:5). In Psalms 118, He is the Deliverer. In Psalms 100, He is greater than David whose line He came from. He is the Victor who would subdue our enemies.

And, He still does!

Yet, Jesus is the rejected king in Psalms 188:22, the rejected cornerstone in Matthew 21:42, forsaken by His friends and sold for a few pieces of silver.

Pilate asked Jesus, *"What is truth?"* The Bible records no answer given by Jesus, except as one can imagine, a look. One can't help but wonder, did Pilate then abruptly leave the conversation, knowing that he was staring Truth in the face? Pilate would never get over it.

Jesus had a human soul and spirit. He groaned at the death of his friend Lazarus (John 11:33) and was troubled at the anticipation of the cross (John 12:27). He felt compassion for people. He wept over the city of Jerusalem. Today, He cries when He witnesses us in travail and He laughs with us when we experience joy and our Spiritual victories.

Jesus became hungry in the wilderness when He was tempted. He became tired in His travels and stopped to rest. He became thirsty in the dry heat of Judea.

Jesus lived, Jesus was rejected, but oh, He was far from done.

Prophesied and Fulfilled: The Death of Jesus

As we sang,
> *"There in the ground His body lay,*
> *Light of the world by darkness slain[1]."*

David depicted the sufferings of Jesus in Psalms 22.
> Verse 1 describes Jesus' cry on the cross, fulfilled in Matthew 27:46.
> Verse 7 tells of the passersby who mocked Him, fulfilled in Matthew 27:39.
> Verse 8 tells the actual words of the insults hurled at Him, fulfilled in Matthew 27:43.
> Verse 16, the piercing of His hands and feet;
> Verse 17, that none of his bones would be broken;
> Verse 18 the soldiers gambling for his clothes and in
> Verse 24, Jesus' cry to His Father, *"Let this cup pass from me; nevertheless not as I will but as thou wilt* (Matthew 26:39).*"* At that moment, Jesus became the Savior, and our Redeemer.

Seven trials Jesus suffered, all illegal, by Annas the former high priest (John 18), by Caiaphas, the high priest (Matthew 26), by the

Sanhedrin (Luke 22), by Pilate, the governor (John 18), by Herod, King of Judea (Luke 23), by Pilate again (Mark 15) and finally by the people themselves (John 19). In Isaiah 52 and 53 are the well-known and myriad prophesies of the sufferings of Christ's violent death, all prophesies fulfilled.

Prophesied and Fulfilled: The Victory of Jesus

And we sang,
> "And as He stands in victory, Sin's curse has lost its grip on me;
> For I am His and He is mine, Bought with the precious blood of Christ[1]."

The apostle Peter applies the Psalmist's hope (Psalms 16:10) to Jesus in Acts 2:2-28, declaring that these verses prophesied that Jesus would be resurrected. David, in Psalms 68:18, predicts the God-ordained ascension and the end of Christ's earthly life. And, oh, how we rejoice and sing of the Mighty Victory at Easter:

> "Up from the grave He arose;
> With a mighty triumph o'er His foes;
> He arose a Victor from the dark domain
> And He lives forever with the saints to reign.
> He arose! He arose! Hallelujah! Christ arose!"[1]

Up from the grave He arose;
With a mighty triumph o'er His foes;
He arose a Victor from the dark domain
And He lives forever with the saints to reign.
He arose! He arose! Hallelujah! Christ arose!"[1]

Jesus died, but then He arose!

The Humanity of Christ

And we sang,
> "*My comforter, my all in all, Here in the love of Christ I stand*[1].*"*

Christ had all human qualities except sin and failure. He was virgin-born and He had a body of flesh and blood. He had a normal childhood development as described in Luke 2:52. I personally believe that Jesus was not skinny and pathetic as some crucifixes depict Him. No, Jesus was the son of a carpenter, who made huge and heavy furniture, wagons and wheels. I can hear Joseph telling him, *"Jesus, take those wheels and put them on Mr. Zechariah's wagon before you finish today..."*

The Bible tells us that Jesus was not necessarily a handsome man who would stand out for his looks, but he must have had a strong body, well-conditioned by hard, physical work, enough to carry a heavy cross up the Via Dolorosa and suffer a long and torturous death.

> *"Down the Via Dolorosa called the way of suffering, like a lamb came the Messiah, Christ the King... He chose to walk that road out of His love for you and me down the Via Dolorosa, all the way to Calvary."*[6]

Jesus was human, but Jesus is... also Divine.

The Deity of Christ

As we sang,
> "*Till on that cross as Jesus died, The wrath of God was satisfied*[1].*"*

Jesus had to be a real man if He was to represent fallen humanity (I John 4:2). If Jesus wasn't a real man, then the death on the cross was an illusion. Jesus demonstrated his humanity on the cross when he refused to succumb to the temptation to call angels to his rescue:

"Stillness filled the Heavens, on Crucifixion day. Some say it rained, I don't know if it's true. Well, I can just imagine if ten thousand angels

cried, that would seem like rain to me and you. The angels all stood ready to take Him from the tree. They waited for the words from His voice. And when He asked the Father 'Why has Thou forsaken Me?' they watched the Savior die of His own choice."[7]

To affirm that Jesus is in fact God is to know that Christ is absolutely equal with the Father in His person and His work. Upon seeing the resurrected Jesus appear in the upper room, Thomas was given an invitation to press his fingers into the fresh wounds of the Savior's side. Do you know the Bible never says that he did? Instead, he fell to his feet and proclaimed *"My Lord and my God* (John 20:28)." Boy, does that tell us something?

In Titus 2:13, Paul refers to Jesus as *"our great God and savior, Jesus Christ."* John refers to Christ as *"the only begotten God..."* Paul also refers to Jesus as Lord in Romans 10:9-13.

Jesus claimed to be the *"Son of God"* on several occasions (John 5:25), equal with God (John 5:18).

Jesus is eternal (John 1:1), omnipresent (John 14:23), omniscient (Matthew 16:21) and omnipotent (Matthew 28:18.

Jesus had all authority of heaven and earth, and the power to forgive sins, something only God can do, therefore Jesus is God (Mark 2:5-10, Isaiah 43:25, 55:7).

Jesus is immutable. He doesn't change, but is forever the same (Hebrews 13:8). That's great news for the Christian, and of course, more proof of His deity.

Jesus is the Creator, and without Him, nothing was made that was made. Likewise, He is the sustainer of all things, the forgiver of sin and the miracle worker. Miracles do happen. Even to people like you and me.

Finally, it is a fundamental truth of Scripture that only God is to be worshiped (Deuteronomy 6:13, 10:20, Matthew 4:10, Acts 10:25-26). Paul tells us that there will be a day when all people in both Earth and Heaven with worship Jesus (Philippians 2:10), Jesus the Deity.

The Hypostatic Union of Christ

As we sang,
> "For ev'ry sin on Him was laid, Here in the death of Christ I live[1].

From a human female and the Holy Spirit of God, came the "hypostatic union" defined as the Second Person. The preincarnate Christ came and took to Himself a human nature and remains forever undiminished Deity and true humanity untied in one person forever.[8]

When Christ came, a person came, not just a nature. Jesus took on an additional nature, a human nature like yours and mine. He didn't simply dwell in a human person. The result of the two natures is the theanthropic Person, the God-Man.

So, Jesus has two distinct natures, deity and humanity. We worship Him as deity and we adore Him as being human like us. There is no intermingling of the two natures, and, as Calvin would attest, the two natures maintain their separate identity[8]. Although He has two natures, Christ is One Person.

The kenosis problem of Philippians 2:7 poses a question: "Of what did Christ empty Himself?" Most kenoticists believe that Christ gave up His sovereign dominion when becoming incarnate. Other kenoticists believe that Christ continued being sovereign while on Earth, but that His divine and human natures were not truly united into one Person. Are they both wrong?

Yes. Surely, they are, for they either diminish the deity of Christ or they undermine the union of the two natures in one Person.

A through study of this doctrinal issue would indicate that, as John Walvoord postulated, Christ merely limited himself to the voluntary non-use of his human attributes.[9] Moreover, Philippians 2:7-8 explains that Jesus took on an additional nature, the form of a bond-slave, just like you and me. Wow! He was made in the likeness of man, was found in the appearance of man, and in that circumstance, He humbled Himself by becoming obedient to the point of death.

He never surrendered His deity for He could not do that.

Jesus' Present Work

As we sang,

> *"Then bursting forth in glorious day, Up from the grave He rose again[1]."*

Christ's works in the New Testament are well chronicled, giving sight to the blind, healing to the lame, raising the dead and raising up the faith of the living. He stilled the storm, fed the 5,000 (more like 12,000 with women and kids) and forgave sin, as only God can do.

In turning water to wine as a favor to His mother at a friend's wedding (John 2:1-11), Jesus brought joy and gladness.

In walking on water and leading Peter to do the same, in producing a catch of fish and stilling the storm, Jesus commanded the elements.

In all of that, Jesus demonstrated that we can do miracles like these and even more. Yes, we can! In John's gospel alone, Jesus' miracles demonstrated His authority over space, time, quality and quantity, nature, misfortune and even death. Jesus told His disciples to *"go and report to John what you hear and see"* (Matthew 11:4).

Jesus came as Israel's Messiah and bore witness to His Messiahship through His words and deeds. In Matthew chapters 5-7, the Bible records Jesus' Sermon On The Mount and His teaching. In chapters 8-10, Jesus performed miracles over various realms as an authentication through his works.

It was obvious that the people had to respond. In chapter 12, the leaders of the Jews declared *"This man casts out demons only by Beezebul [Satan] the ruler of demons* (Matthew 12:24)." Thus, Israel rejected Jesus and Jesus was crucified.

Jesus' death was "substitutionary," in that he died a substitution for you and me. His death was vicarious, done in our stead. Either way, Jesus' death provided redemption for our sins and those of the world. First Corinthians 6:20 states that we have been *"bought with a price."* The word for "bought" is the Greek *agorazo*, which pictures a slave being purchased in the ancient public slave market. Jesus bought me out of the slave market and set me free.

Walk with Jesus

Moreover, when Jesus died, He reconciled us to God and gave us peace with God.

Jesus' death is also called "propitiation," meaning that the righteous demands of a holy God were met. We are forgiven and justified, *just as if* we had never sinned.

> *Christ's death is meaningless without His resurrection.*

Make no mistake: Christ's death is meaningless without His resurrection. Paul tells us, *"If Christ has not been raised, your faith is worthless [and] you are still in your sins* (I Corinthians 15:17)."

So,

    Christ's resurrection validates our faith.

    Christ's resurrection guarantees God's acceptance of Christ's work.

    Christ's resurrection was essential, because the Holy Spirit (the Comforter) could only come if Christ would depart (John 16:7).

    Christ's resurrection fulfilled the prophesies of his purpose.

    Christ's resurrection was proven by the empty tomb.

Christ's resurrection was proven by the shape of the linen wrappings discovered after He had left. I once heard a story that, when dining, it was customary to leave the table and dispose of what had been eaten, to come back and eat more. Such was a compliment to the host. To indicate that the guest was not through with the meal occasion, he would fold the napkin and set it at his place, indicating that he'd be back. When the wrappings of Jesus were found, the linen cloth that had wrapped His head was found neatly folded. Only Jesus could have folded it. What was Jesus telling us? *"I will be back. Save my place!"* Wow!

> *"I will be back. Save my place!"*
> *Jesus*

Christ's resurrection was proven by His appearances:

    the women at the tomb,

    Peter and John racing to the burial place and discovering Him gone, the two who walked with Jesus on the road to Emmaus, and

the conversion experience of Saul who became Paul.

After His resurrection, Jesus was seen by as many as five hundred people in a single occasion. Knowledge of the resurrection inspired His disciples to live for Him, to accomplish great works and to perform wonderful ministries far and wide. Jesus still inspires today!

Christ's resurrection was proven by the sending of the Holy Spirit at Pentecost, witnessed by many. After His ascension, Christ's glory was no longer veiled. He is now high and lifted up, exalted and enthroned in Heaven.

Jesus' Future Work

And we sang,
> "No pow'r of Hell, no scheme of man, Can ever pluck me from His hand;
> Till He returns or calls me home, Here in the pow'r of Christ I'll stand[1]."

Jesus is truly our King as He was prophesied in Genesis 49:10 and II Samuel 7:16.

He is the Prophet, the ultimate fulfilment of the position. No single prophet completely revealed the will of the Father except Jesus Christ (John 1:18).

Jesus is the High Priest, according to the order of Melchizadek in Hebrews 5:6-10, 6:20, 7:11 and 7:17. He continually represents us as believers because He lives forever (Hebrews 7:24). He completely saves us because His intercession never ceases (Hebrews 7:25). He has no personal sins to impede His work as our priest (Hebrews 7:27) and He finished His work with one grand offering (Hebrews 10:12).

Jesus is prophet, priest and king. These three offices of Christ are keys to the purpose of His incarnation.

His prophetic office revealed God's message.

His priestly office saves and intercedes and in

His kingly office, He reigns over the entire world.

The divine juxtaposition of all three offices are culminated in the Lord Jesus Christ.

The hope exhibited in the Scriptures is the ultimate restoration of all things under the Messiah. He is coming again to rescue His people and inaugurate a millennial reign in Glory.

The Forever Reign of Jesus

And we sang,
> "What heights of love, what depths of peace,
> When fears are stilled, when strivings cease.
> No guilt in life, no fear in death, This is the pow'r of Christ in me;
> From life's first cry to final breath, Jesus commands my destiny[1]."

Psalms 2:6-9 promises you and me that Christ will become King in Jerusalem, ruling over the nations of the world. He will reign over a kingdom of justice and peace (Isaiah 11:1-16, Daniel 7:13-14 and Zechariah 14:9-21).

"My hope is built on nothing less than Jesus' blood and righteousness. I dare not trust the sweetest frame, but wholly lean on Jesus' Name."[10]

The best mathematical equation ever made: 1 cross + 3 nails = 4 given.

On Christ the Solid Rock, I stand.

> *"Light of the world, Emanuel,*
> *The Word of God has come to dwell,*
> *Our only hope, is in a Child,*
> *Let God and sinners now be reconciled...*
> *The lame will walk, the blind will see,*
> *The captive heart will be set free.*
> *A Child has come to change the world forever*
> *No more will sin or sorrow reign, a King has come to save the day.*
> *A Light has dawned, and darkness is over.*

12 Ways to Walk with God

> *Glory, glory, we have our Savior,*
> *Glory, glory to our God.*
> *Peace on Earth is born in a manger,*
> *For Love has come to us,*
> *We have our Savior."*[11]

---

[1] Lyrics from *"In Christ Alone,"* Words and Music by Keith Getty & Stuart Townend, © 2001 Kingsway Thankyou Music, performed by Morning Star Records recording artists, *Buddy Merrick & Praise.*

[2] Sanders, J. Oswald, *The Incomparable Christ* (Chicago, IL: Moody Publishers, 2009)

[3] The list goes on, of course. These words taken from the song, *"Jesus Is... In Every Book of The Bible,"* © and (p) 1990, by Morning Star Music, as written and recorded by Buddy Merrick and *Buddy Merrick & Praise*. All rights reserved.

[4] Buswell, J. Oliver, *A Systematic Theology Of The Christian Religion* (Grand Rapids: Zondervan, 1962), 1:33.

[5] Enns, Paul, *The Moody Handbook of Theology* (Chicago: Moody Publishers, 2008), pg. 233.

[6] From the song, *"Via Dolorosa,"* words and music by Billy Sprague and Niles Borop, © 1963, EMI Christian Music Publishing, as sung by Sandi Patti (Word Music).

[7] From the gospel song, *10,000 Angels Cried,* © 1999 by Fortune City, written & played by David Patillo.

[8] Enns, *Moody Handbook of Theology,* pg. 238.

[9] Walvoord, John F., *Jesus Christ Our Lord* (Chicago: Moody, 1964), pg. 114.

[10] Lyrics from the hymn, *"My Hope is Built on Nothing Less"* by Edward Mote, 1797-1874, as published in *The Lutheran Hymnal* (St. Louis: Concordia Publishing House, 1941). The text is taken from I Timothy 1:1.

[11] Lyrics from the song, *"We have Our Savior,"* sung by Buddy Merrick at Parkside Baptist Church, in the Christmas musical by the same name, directed by Dave Purkey. Alice McBride said, *"This was the best song in the whole musical, because of it's message!"* (Franklin, TN: Brentwood Benson Publishing, 2011).

Hyprstatic union (handwritten)

VI. Walk with the Holy Spirit

Pneumatology - Is the Holy Spirit a thing or is it a Him?

Preface

"What's this thing called the Holy Spirit?"

Pneumatology is the study of the doctrine of the Holy Spirit, which of course, is also then, a study of God and Jesus Christ, inasmuch as the Holy Spirit is the Third Person of the triune nature of God.

First, and important, let's be clear: The Holy Spirit, has personality or personhood. So, He is a *He*, not an *it!*

He is deity.

>In Scripture, He is represented in many ways, in revelation and inspiration.

>He relates to Jesus and Jesus' work in profound collaboration.

>He works in baptism, in sealing our salvation and in bestowing spiritual gifts, abilities and missions to us.

The Bible tells us that the Holy Spirit searches all things (II Corinthians 2:10). He examines the depths of God and reveals Him to us believers.

Galatians 5:25 exhorts us, *"If we live in the Spirit, let us also walk in the Spirit."* That should be our

Walk in the Holy Spirit. You were born to enjoy perfection.

1 Corn. 15:8 (handwritten)

12 Ways to Walk with God

desire and with the help of the Holy Spirit, the Comforter, we seek to walk in His ways. Walk With God. Walk in the Holy Spirit. You were born to enjoy perfection.

The Personhood of the Holy Spirit

To understand and relate to the Holy Spirit, one must understand that the Holy Spirit, as a Person, has intellect, emotions and will. Rejected by the Jehovah's Witnesses, the Holy Spirit is much more than a mere *"influence emanating from the Father"* as they believe.

As a mere human, we don't have the ability to fully understand God. When Moses was on the mountain, where He was given the Ten Commandments, he heard God speak out of a burning bush. But, the bush was not consumed by the fire. Before Moses could turn to see why the bush didn't burn up, "God called unto him" (Exodus 3:4) and stopped him from coming closer. Now, the Buddy Merrick version says that God told Moses, *"Don't look at me, because if you do, your head will blow up."* OK, that's not scriptural, but it's close. It's why God then told Moses to take off his shoes, to yield all authority to God in that place. God in all His Holiness, is incomprehensible to a mere man. We couldn't absorb all His glory in a single look. Without knowing the "why," we need to yield and trust Him. That I understand.

So, the Holy Spirit reveals the Father to us, in doses and ways that we *can* handle. Even as the Holy Spirit knows the Father, so the Father knows the mind of the Spirit, says Romans 8:27. The word *mind* in the Greek is *phronema*, meaning "the way of thinking, mind-set, aim, aspiration and striving."[1] So, obviously the Holy Spirit is a Person with intellect.

Ephesians 4:30 commands us not to grieve the Holy Spirit. How do we do that? By lying, by being angry, by stealing, by being lazy or by speaking an unkind word (Ephesians 25- 29). Only a "person" can be grieved, not a mere "influence," folks. The Person of the Holy Spirit can be grieved.

The Holy Spirit distributes spiritual gifts as He wills.[2] The same Greek phrase is used in James 1:8, to describe the will of God the Father.

The Holy Spirit teaches us. Jesus told us He would send another helper, in the Holy Spirit, that is of the same caliber of Christ. John tells us that the Holy Spirit will teach us (John 14:26), and even better than most teachers, this one will actually cause us to remember what we are taught of Christ! Wow, wish I could do that!

The Holy Spirit testifies to us about Jesus (John 15:26).

The Holy Spirit will guide us into all truth (John 16:13).

The Holy Spirit will convict us, acting as a divine prosecutor in convincing us of sin, righteousness and judgment.

The Holy Spirit will regenerate us. Just as Jesus gave me life, the Holy Spirit regenerates life.

The Holy Spirit will intercede for us in our times of weakness (Romans 8:26). All things work together for good in our life (Romans 8:28) because the Holy Spirit intercedes for us. Again, only a person can intercede, an influence can't.

The Holy Spirit will direct us. In Acts 16:6, the Holy Spirit exercised His will in forbidding Paul to preach in Asia and redirecting Paul to minister in Europe. He will lead us in the same way.

Finally, the Holy Spirit commands and guides our actions and directions (Acts 13:4).

So, like the Father, the Holy Spirit can be grieved, blasphemed (Matthew 12:32), resisted (Acts 7:51), and lied to, as in the story of the deceit of Ananias and Sapphira in Acts 5:3. When we obey the leading of the Holy Spirit, we obey the Father. They are one in the same, and the benefits of understanding that Leadership are the same.

The Deity of the Holy Spirit

The Holy Spirit has Life in Himself (Romans 8:2).

He is omniscient (I Corinthians 2:10-12), infinitely wise and all-knowing. He knows about God, about the things of which man finds *unsearchable* and *unfathomable* (Romans 11:33).

He is omnipotent (Job 33:4), having unlimited power. In the creation account of Genesis 1:2, the Holy Spirit is seen hovering over the creation as a hen over its young; the Holy Spirit gave life to creation.[3]

He is omnipresent (Psalms 139:7-10; John 14:17), there at all places at the same time. The Psalmist tells us that we can't escape the presence of the Holy Spirit. The Savior tells us that we will be indwelt with His presence.

He is eternal (Hebrews 9:14), as God, with no beginning and no end.

He is holy (Matthew 12:32). While we sometimes refer to Him as the Spirit, He is in truth the Holy Spirit. As the Third Person of the Trinity, he possesses this transcendent attribute of deity.

He is Love (Galatians 5:22). If He did not possess love of the same kind as Jesus and God, He could not produce love in a believer like He does.

He is Truth (John 14:17). Jesus tells us that we know Him, the Holy Spirit. He dwells in us and shall continuously dwell in us. That's awesome news.

The Work of the Holy Spirit

The overshadowing of Mary by the Holy Spirit in Matthew 1:20 was the means by which Jesus became a human being. He became incarnate when His eternal Person took on the human form. The Holy Spirit caused the humanity of Christ to originate and that is His [the Holy Spirit's] act of "generation."[4]

The Holy Spirit is the author of new birth. John 6:44 tells us that no man comes to the Savior unless the Father who sent Jesus draws him. Later in the same chapter (verses 63-65), Jesus explains that, *"It is the Spirit who gives life; the flesh profits nothing; the words that I have spoken to you are spirit and are life."* So, it is the Holy Spirit who draws one to God and it is He who "re-generates" a person.

The Holy Spirit inspired Scripture. He superintended the writers to guarantee an inerrant Scripture. II Timothy 3:16 tells us that the work of the Holy Spirit in this manner is the same as that of the Father.

The Holy Spirit sanctifies us unto Christ (I Corinthians 1:30, Hebrews 10:14-15 and I Peter 1:2).

The Holy Spirit is called alongside us to be our advocate or *paraclete*. It was the Holy Spirit who descended on Jesus like a dove, and He clothes us in the same fashion. At Pentecost tongues of fire fell on the apostles notating God's approval of them. There's no doubt that the Holy Spirit will guide any believer in God's ministry.

We're never alone! The Holy Spirit is with us!

Oil, Water and Wind

Oil is a type of the Holy Spirit inasmuch as the Old Testament practice of anointing priests and kinds served as a type of ministry of the Holy Spirit. Oil depicted the Holy Spirit's power in strengthening Zerubbabel and Joshua to lead the people in completing the construction of the temple in 515 BC. *"Not by might nor by power, but by my Spirit (Zechariah 4:6)."*

You know that kings in ancient times sealed their documents and letters with a drop of wax and an official seal, right? Likewise, the Holy Spirit is the means whereby God presses His official seal on us. Through the sealing of the Holy Spirit we are secure in our salvation and in our place in God's Kingdom, because we are officially sealed.

Water is a type of the Holy Spirit, too, as Jesus proclaimed, *"If anyone is thirsty, let him come to me and drink. He who believes in me, as the Scripture said, from his inner being will flow rivers of living water* (John 7:37-38)." In the next verse John explains that, *"He spoke of the Holy Spirit."* Water is an emblem of eternal life and a reception of the Holy Spirit.

Wind may be translated as "spirit" from the Greek *pneuma,* from which we get our commonly used word *pneumatic,* meaning driven by wind or air as in pneumatic tires for our car. Jesus used this attribute of the Holy Spirit to explain the meaning of being born again. He said, *"The wind bloweth where it listeth, and thou hearest the sound thereof, but canst tell whence it cometh, and wither it goeth; so is every one that is born of the Spirit."* Likewise, no one dictates to the wind (I Corinthians 12:11).

Thus we have "pneuma-tology," the study of the doctrine of the Holy Spirit.

The Holy Spirit in Revelation and Inspiration

The Old Testament prophet's message of revelation did not originate with himself. He was merely the vessel through whom the Holy Spirit spoke, revealed and inspired.

He did so by the spoken word (Genesis 18:13,17).

He did so by dreams such as those dreamed by Abimelech (Genesis 20:3), Jacob (31:10-13), Joseph (37:5-9) and Nebuchandnezzar in Daniel chapter two.

He did so through visions as experienced by Abraham (Genesis 15:1), Nathan (I Chronicles 17:15), Ezekiel (Ezekiel 1:1) and Daniel (Daniel 8:1).

He did so in theophanies, or physical manifestations of God, as experienced by Abraham (Genesis 18), Joshua (Joshua 5:14) and Gideon (Judges 6:22).

The Ministry of the Holy Spirit in the Old Testament

The Old Testament believer was regenerated by the Holy Spirit (Psalms 51:10). Likewise, in John 14:16, Jesus revealed that following Pentecost, a new ministry would be done by the Holy Spirit, an indwelling versus the Spirit in the past which was simply being with them.

This past dwelling was selective and temporary, more for a specific task.

This new indwelling is permanent and eternal, as in forever!

The Ministry of the Holy Spirit in the New Testament

The ministry of the Holy Spirit in the New Testament reveals how the Holy Spirit ministered to and through Jesus. He of course, was the agent of the virgin birth of a sinless man, with human limitations as a human.

In Luke 4:18, the Holy Spirit anointed Christ, fulfilling the prophesy of Isaiah 61:1. The act of anointing conferred power. In this case, the anointing empowered Christ for ministry.

In a believer, the Holy Spirit anoints us to Walk With God, for ministry, to love another and to seek God's will and direction in our life. The Holy Spirit's anointing empowers us to do things we can't even imagine having the power to do, and in doing them, to accomplish God's work in our life.

The Holy Spirit filled Christ and He filled every believer and still does. Luke 4:1 attests to Jesus being *"full of the Holy Spirit... [and] led around by the Spirit."* The entire life of Jesus was bound up with the Holy Spirit from His birth to His death and resurrection.[6] Likewise, when we are yielded to the Holy Spirit, He can possess us fully and, in that sense, fill us (Romans 8:9 and Ephesians 1:13-14).

> *Being filled with the Spirit, we have freedom for Him to occupy every part of our life.*

Being filled with the Spirit, we have freedom for Him to occupy every part of our life, guiding and controlling us every day. His power is exerted through us so that what we do is fruitful to God. The filling of the Spirit does not apply to outward acts alone; it also applies to the innermost thoughts and motives of our actions as well. As Psalm 19:14 says, *"May the words of my mouth and the meditation of my heart be pleasing in your sight, oh Lord, my Rock and my Redeemer."*

If we sin against the Holy Spirit, by
    quenching Him (I Thessalonians 5:19) or
    by grieving Him (Ephesians 4:30) or
    even - God forbid - by blaspheming Him (Matthew

12:24,31-32), we sin against our Savior and against God, and we declare that Jesus is not the Son of God. Having witnessed the power, love and work of God through Jesus, we would then be ascribing His work to the devil, thus we'd be rejecting and even blaspheming Him.

In rejecting the Holy Spirit and Jesus, we would commend ourselves to Hell, with no opportunity for pardon. So how do we guard against such actions? Our protection from such a heinous act, is God's ownership of us. God is a merciful God and well acquainted with our heart. We can never envision our self committing such a sin because our faith and love would not allow it. It's impossible, for we have the Love of Jesus within us and the empowering and guidance of the Holy Spirit directing our every move.

Praise the Holy Spirit! He is our Sustainer!

The Baptism of the Holy Spirit

First, one must understand that the baptism of the Holy Spirit is unique to the church age. The baptism of the Holy Spirit began at Pentecost. The baptism of the Holy Spirit includes all believers (I Corinthians 12:13). It brings believers into union with other believers and into union with Jesus. The baptism of the Holy Spirit is not experiential and can't be prayed for.

> *The baptism of the Holy Spirit is not experiential and can't be prayed for.*

For some charismatic churches, can I repeat that? The baptism of the Holy Spirit is not experiential and can't be prayed for. Here's what that means:

It's important to distinguish the *indwelling* from the *infilling* of the Spirit.

The permanent indwelling of the Spirit is not for a select few believers, but for all believers. There are a number of references in Scripture that support this conclusion.

The Holy Spirit is a gift given to all believers in Jesus without exception, and no conditions are placed upon this gift except faith in Christ (John 7:37-39).

The Holy Spirit is given at the moment of salvation (Ephesians 1:13). The Bible in Galatians 3:2 emphasizes this same truth, saying that the sealing and indwelling of the Spirit took place at the time of believing.

The Holy Spirit *indwells* believers permanently. The Holy Spirit is given to believers as a down payment, or verification of their future glorification in Christ according to II Corinthians 1:22 and Ephesians 4:30.[7] There are no exceptions or conditions attached except faith in Jesus (John 7:37-39). It's up to the believer to simply accept the gift as one does when accepting the precious Gift of Salvation from our Lord and Savior Jesus Christ.

Then, too, Ephesians 5:18 commands that we be *filled* with the Spirit. However, praying for the filling of the Holy Spirit as some Pentecostalists and Charismatics do, does not accomplish the filling. Only our obedience to God's commands allows the Spirit freedom to work within us.

So if the charismatic or Pentecostal want to pray to receive the infilling of the Holy Spirit, for himself or another, then the prayer should be for the faith to receive what God has already promised us. The Charismatics and Pentecostals are right in that some do not exercise the infilling of the Holy Spirit because their faith does not allow them to. Praying for that faith is a perfectly wonderful thing to do.

The gift is given at salvation, therefore by deduction, the unbeliever does not possess the gift or sealing of the Holy Spirit. That is why he or she is said to be lost. Romans 8:9 says, *"If anyone does not have the Spirit of Christ, he does not belong to Him."*

Lost people don't have the gift. Jude 19 refers to lost people and their focus on the sensual things of life as devoid of the Spirit. "<u>Clark's Commentary On The Bible</u>" says they are, *"guided simply by their own lusts and passions, their bible being the devices and covetousness of their own hearts; for they have not the Spirit - they are not spiritually minded; and have no Holy Ghost, no inspiration from God."*[5]

The Gifts of the Spirit

There are two Greek words used to describe Gifts of the Spirit, *pneumatikos* and *charisma*.

Pneumatikos means "spiritual things" or "things pertaining to the Spirit." These gifts are not natural talents but have their origin with the Holy Spirit and are given to a believer by the Holy Spirit (I Corinthians 12:11).

Charisma gifts are "grace gifts," a gift that is not a naturally developed ability but rather a gift bestowed on a believer (I Corinthians 12:4), a divine endowment of a special ability for service upon a member of the body of Christ.[8]

Concerning gifts, the Bible says, *"And He gave some apostles; and some, prophets; and some evangelists; and some pastors and teachers; for the perfection of the saints, for the work of the ministry, for the edifying of the body of Christ"* (Ephesians 4:11).

"Apostles" were representatives of Christ in the early church. They performed signs and wonders, were witnesses to the resurrection and were given to the church only at the beginning (Ephesians 2:20). They received direct revelation from the Lord but they were not appointed after the time of Paul (I Corinthians 15:8).

"Prophets" (Romans 12:6) proclaimed a divine revelation, revealed hidden things, and foretold the future. Since the revelation came from God it was true, therefore the test of being a true prophet was in the accuracy of the prophecy. Again, because the foundation of the church has been laid, there is no need for the gift of prophesy today.

The gift of "Miracles" was given to authenticate a message and God enabled His messengers to validate the new message the apostles preached. With the completion of the canon of Scripture, the need for miracles as a validating sign disappeared. Although the gift of miracles ceased with the Apostles, God still performs miracles as an answer to prayer.

Paul tells us, in I Corinthians 12:8-10, of different gifts of the Holy Spirit, *"For to one is given by the Spirit the word of wisdom; to another the word of knowledge by the same Spirit; to another faith by the same Spirit; to another the gift of healing by the same Spirit; to another the working of miracles; to another prophesy; to another discerning of spirits; to another divers kinds of tongues; to another the interpretation of tongues."*

The gift of miracles is not the gift of "healing." An examination of New Testament healings by Christ and the apostles shows that they were:

instantaneous (Mark 1:42),
complete (Matthew 14:36),
permanent (Matthew 14:36),
limited to needs of the day such as leprosy (Mark 1:40),
unconditional (John 9:25),
purposeful and
not just for the purpose of relieving people from their suffering (Luke 5:15-16),
subordinate, that is secondary to the preaching of the Word (Luke 9:6),
significant, that is, meant to confirm Jesus and His message (John 3:2),
successful (Matthew 17:20) and
inclusive (Mark 5:39-43).
God still heals as an answer to prayer.

The gift of *"tongues"* did not involve a babbling in an unknown language. Acts 2:6, 8 and 11 establishes that Biblical tongues were languages. When the foreign Jews visited Jerusalem at Pentecost, they heard the apostles proclaim the good news in their native language or tongue.

Too, there is no evidence that the "tongues" of Corinthians were different than the ones of Acts. Tongues was a temporary and lesser gift (I Corinthians 12:28), and meant to authenticate the gospel.

Likewise the gift of "interpretation of tongues" involved the supernatural ability of someone in the assembly to interpret the foreign language spoken by the one who had the gift of tongues. The Charismatics today adopt this phenomenon as a basis for their worship in church, and while some churches create rules for when and how tongues may

12 Ways to Walk with God

be used, it's commonplace for a preacher to "break out in tongues" as either an emphasis for a point in preaching or a demonstration of communication with God. Sorry, but neither is Biblically accurate.

The gift of "evangelism," or proclaiming the Good News, involves a burden for the lost and an ability to present a clear explanation of Christ's redemption, sin, the substitutionary death of Christ, faith, forgiveness and reconciliation in a way that can be received by an unbeliever. Despite the level of his talent, no carefully-derived presentation will bear fruit unless the Holy Spirit empowers the evangelist, and that's true either one-on-one or while preaching to the masses. The gift of evangelism that the Holy Spirit gave to that preacher should be a testimony of what Christ did and how the presence of the Holy Spirit guides and helps him every day. Such is the greatest presentation of the gospel.

> *No carefully-derived presentation will bear fruit unless the Holy Spirit empowers the evangelist.*

When I was preaching in Hawai'i, I came across a group of beach-dwellers who were commonly called "beach people." They were unkept, disheveled and dirty except for what the ocean would do for them by swimming or surfing in it. They lived on the beach, literally, with no means of support, except by begging and stealing or diving in the city's trash cans. Sex of course was free.

Interestingly, a key component to their comradery was constantly reading and carrying the Bible. It offered a bit of legitimacy to their philosophy. One beach person actually argued with me about Scriptures he'd found about God making grass, and offered it to me as a rationale to legitimizing his use of marijuana. Oh, how I wanted to debate that, but I thought it would be useless to try, so I didn't.

To minister to these people obviously entailed an understanding of their lifestyle, even if one disapproved of it. Because I was among the few who reached out to them, I found myself with a Sunday School class at Waikiki Baptist Church, much to the complete chagrin of elders and the tourist worshipers who came in their Sunday best. With these people among them, the church leaders saw their decades of ministry

Walk with the Holy Spirit

going down the drain! So, our fellowship was relegated the church's kitchen, because it has a separate entrance, and so the beach people's appearance wouldn't hamper the worship experience desired by the general congregation.

As you can imagine, the hardest thing to do was to present the Scripture, because these people knew the Word. They mangled it's meaning, but they knew it so well they could defend any position any way they wanted. Unless one was as really familiar with the Word - or, better yet, was led by the Holy Spirit - getting God's point across was a chore. Through that God-given experience, I learned two big things:

First, know the Word. And if one argues with you, tell the Truth, do your best, pray that it's best and let Jesus do the rest. God can handle dissenters much better than you can. And you'll be surprised what the Holy Spirit can do, given an opportunity!

> *Do your best, pray that it's best, and let Jesus do the rest.*

Second, know that the finest Bible expositor in the world can't dispute your own testimony! That's yours and yours alone, given to you as a "special revelation," a gift from the Holy Spirit. So, tell 'em what God has done in your life. It's irrefutable! That's one point you will win, guaranteed!

Through it all, it was amazing how many beach people came to truly know the Lord as Messiah, Savior and Lord, cleaned up and joined the congregation, usually on the front row! Praise God! How 'bout that? And the great hearts of that wonderful fellowship at Waikiki Baptist Church? They not only accepted them, they even enjoyed their believer's baptism with them. God is so good!

By the way, the Bible says that all believers are to do the work of an evangelist (II Timothy 4:5). All means all and that's all that all means!

The gift of *"teaching"* for a pastor-teacher has a clear analogy in the Bible with that of a shepherd as well as an ability to teach (Romans 12:7 and I Corinthians 12:29). A teacher has a great interest in the Word of God. He is disciplined to study the word and then to communicate the Word to people. Teaching requires development. Teaching is not a natural talent and it can't be accomplished by mere uneducated or unprepared off-the cuff bellowing.

To preach "as the Spirit leads" is too often an excuse for unpreparedness and as such it is an insult to both the Lord and the congregation. On the other hand, the Holy Spirit can make the most mediocre of teachers into a virtual Billy Graham! It's amazing how many people tell me what a fantastic seminar we just had, when I left the room feeling quite the failure!

The gift of *"service"* in Romans 12:7 is revealed in the Greek word *diakonia* meaning to minister to others. A true minister meets others at the point of their need and does so above himself. Do you remember the example in the movie, *"Evan Almighty"* where Morgan Freeman, playing God, instructs Steve Carell (as a reluctantly obedient ark-builder) that the purpose of his difficult and complicated experience was *"A.R.K.,"* or *"one Act of Random Kindness at a time?"* It reminded us that a simple act of kindness is indeed service to the King, as small as it may seem.

> *Morgan Freeman told us that "You can change the world, with one act of random kindness (A.R.K.) at a time."*

The ministry of *"helps"* is similar to service. The cartoon character "Maxine" asks *"If it's true that we are here to help others, then what exactly are the others here for?"* She's kind of right, isn't she? The truth is, we are *all* called by God to render random acts of kindness. That's living in the character of Jesus, striving for His righteousness, and that kind of service is something all Christians are called to do. Walk With God in service.

"Faith" is a gift (I Corinthians 12:9) that needs to be shared. All Christians have saving faith, but only some have the gift of faith which manifests itself in unusual deeds of trust. This person has the capacity to see something that needs to be done and to believe God will do it through him, eves though it looks impossible.[9]

My wife Carol, says my greatest gift is that of "exhortation," building up another in the Name of Christ and by the power of the Holy Spirit.

Walk with the Holy Spirit

Exhortation involves edifying, getting another to act, and sometimes involves consolation and comforting.

Carol's gift, the gift of "mercy," is showing compassion toward the sick, poor or needy, out of a gladness to help.

The gift of "giving" means to share with someone. Paul tells us to give liberally (Philippians 4:10-16). In my own walk, I began to give more liberally when I discovered that all I had belonged to Christ anyway. Hey, we're not the owner of our checkbook, we're only the check-writer and we write as He instructs us to do. In my business, I had also found that Christ will not allow my failure and will likewise instruct me regarding my expenses - and my giving.

The gift of "discerning spirits" was terminated at the canon of Scripture. The word itself should discern the authenticity of a revelation. A former pastor of mine told me, *"if it doesn't feel like it's true, it probably isn't."* Look it up!

The gift of "administration" is the ability to lead.

The gift of "wisdom" stands first in the list of gifts because it is the whole system of revealed truth, the capacity to receive this revealed truth from God and present it to the people of God.[10] Because this gift is related to receiving and transmitting direct revelation from God, the gift has ceased with the completion of the canon of Scripture.

Should we seek spiritual gifts?

The gift of "knowledge" appears to be closely related to the gift of wisdom and refers to the ability to properly understand the truths revealed to the apostles and prophets.[11]

Finally, is the question: "Should we seek gifts?" The apostle Paul's greatest comment concerning gifts was written in I Corinthians 12:31. Here, he said, *"But eagerly desire the greater gifts. And now I will show you the most excellent way."*

If one reads on to include I Corinthians 13:1-2 in Paul's instruction, the Bible is very clear that the most excellent way is love. No surprise, right? It's the greatest fruit of the Spirit. Love should be pursued before and during our pursuit of any other gifts from God. Later, in I

Corinthians 14:1, Paul continues to instruct us to learn to *"follow the way of love"* while we *"eagerly desire spiritual gifts."* (NIV).

Seek the best gift? Yes. But, understand that the best gift is love. All other gifts should be prayerfully left to the Holy Spirit's direction as we draw closer to Jesus Christ.

Summary

The Holy Spirit enables us to be victorious in the Christian life. The apostle Paul admonished us Christians to *"walk by the spirit,"* to conduct our lives under the power and influence of the Holy Spirit and to let the inward impulses of the Holy Spirit continue to control our behavior. This is our duty as born-again Christians.

The Holy Spirit is the source of all good and gracious impulses in our life. He works within us, teaches us, intercedes in our prayers, inspires us, and gives us wisdom and direction. By His help and power, we can live and overcome the inevitable temptations, sorrows and sadness in our life and turn them into joy.

We are loved by the Holy Spirit just as we are loved by Jesus and the Father.

Even having studied in-depth the different gifts of the Spirit, I do not seek certain gifts or pray for them, but I seek to love others with what I have, that is, a complete infilling and indwelling of the Holy Spirit to guide me in my Walk With God. It's what the Bible tells us to do.

The Bible in Romans 8:4 tells us to *"walk after the Spirit, so that the requirement of the Law might be fulfilled in us, who do not walk according to the flesh but according to the Spirit."* We can't win the spiritual victory by our own personal strength or will power, but we can pray and we can walk in the Spirit.

So, let's sing,
> *Holy Spirit rain down, rain down*
> *Oh Comforter and Friend,*
> *How we need Your touch again.*

Holy Spirit rain down, rain down,
Let Your power fall,
Let Your voice be heard.
Come and change our hearts
As we stand on Your word.
Holy Spirit rain down.
No eye has seen, no ear has heard,
No mind can know what God has in store,
So open up Heaven, open it wide
Over Your church and over our lives.
Holy Spirit, rain down, on me.[12]

---

[1] Arndt William F., and Gingrich, F. Wilbur, *A Greek-English Lexicon of the New Testament and Other Early Christian Literature*, rev. F. Wilbur Gingrich and Frederick W. Danker (Chicago: University of Chicago, 1979), pg. 866.

[2] The phrase, "Just as He will," *kathos bouletai*, stands in the emphatic position in the Greek text drawing attention to the fact that the Holy Spirit *does just as He wills.*

[3] Keil, C. F. and Delitzsch, F., *Biblical Commentary on the Old Testament*, 24 viols. (Reprint. Grand Rapids, Eerdmans, 1968), 1:149.

[4] Chafer, Lewis Sperry, *Systematic Theology*, 8 viols. (Dallas: Dallas Seminary, 1948), 6:33.

[5] Clarke, Adam (1762-1832), *Clarke's Commentary On The Bible* (Thomas Nelson, 1997).

[6] Robertson, A.T., *Word Pictures in the New Testament*, 10 viols. (Nashville: Broadman, 1930), 2:48.

[7] Stanley, Charles, *The Wonderful Spirit-Filled Life* (Thomas Nelson, 1995). I had the privilege of performing in concert at First Baptist Church of Atlanta and spending some time with Dr. Stanley. As the former president of the Southern Baptist Convention, he is the kindest man and the epitome of sound doctrine of the Southern Baptist belief.

[8] McRae, William, *The Dynamics of Spiritual Gifts* (Grand Rapids: Zondervan, 1976), pg. 18.

[9] Ibid, pg. 66.

12 Ways to Walk with God

[10] Ibid, pg. 65.

[11] Hodge, Charles, *First Corinthians* (Crossway Books, 1995), pg. 246.

[12] From the song, *"Rain Down,"* by Russell Fragar, © 1997 by Hillsong Music, Australia.

VII. Walk with God

Theology Proper - Is God really real?

Preface

Someone once said, "God loves everyone, but probably prefers fruits of the spirit over being nuts about your religion."

What do we really know about God?

God Himself tells us, in Jeremiah 9:23-24, *"Thus smith the Lord: 'Let not a wise man boast of his wisdom, and let not the mighty man boast of his might, let not a rich man boast of his riches; but let him who boasts boast of this, that he understands and knows Me, that I am the Lord who exercises lovingkindness, justice, and righteousness on Earth; for I delight in these things,' declares the Lord."*

The ultimate success story begins with finding and knowing God.

"Theology Proper" is what we call a study of the doctrine of God.

The Bible gives witness to two facts regarding the knowledge of God.

First, it teaches us that God is "incomprehensible," and then it also tells us that God is "knowable." Both are true, of course, but not in an absolute sense.

To say that God is incomprehensible simply means that a finite person like me can't know everything there is to know about God who is an infinite being. God's incomprehensibility is declared in passages like Job 11:7 and Isaiah 40:18.

To say that God is knowable means that, though incomprehensible, God can be known and I can grow in the knowledge of God, at least in a limited sense and to the degree that is needed for me to trust God and have a personal and growing relationship with Him.

Jesus tells me in His Word that He is knowable: John 14:7 says, *"If you had known Me, you would have known My Father also; from now on you know Him, and have seen Him."*

And, in John 17:3, Jesus prayed to our Father, *"And this is eternal life, that they may know Thee, the only true God, and Jesus Christ whom Thou hast sent."* In other words, knowing God is knowing eternal life. OK, we can understand that. That's good.

In his wonderful book, *"Knowing God"*, J. I. Packer writes: *"The world becomes a strange, mad and painful place and life in it is a disappointing and unpleasant business for those who do not know about God. Disregard the study of God, and you sentence yourself to stumble and blunder through life blindfold as it were, with no sense of direction and no understanding of what surrounds you. This way you can waste your life and lose your soul.*[1]

The Existence of God

The "cosmological argument" for the existence of God stems from the concept that something can't come from nothing, therefore there must be an original cause for the world's existence. That, or He, is God.

The "teleological argument" for the existence of God says that since the universe is characterized by order and harmony, there must be a master architect. The psalmist sees the magnificence of God's creation and recognizes that it testifies to His existence (Psalms 8:3-4 and 19:1-4).

The "anthropological argument" for the existence of God sees man as created in the image of God (Genesis 1:26-28). The image of God in man is spiritual, not physical (Ephesians 4:24; Colossians 3:10). Man isn't simply a physical being but also a moral being with conscience, intellect, emotion and will. A blind force or happenstance couldn't create a man with all these attributes.

The "moral argument" for the existence of God goes on to say that everyone has an awareness of right and wrong and a sense of morality. Man, unlike other forms of being, has moral standards. Only man is capable of righteousness, even the righteousness of Jesus.

Finally, the "ontological argument" for the existence of God reasons that if man could conceive of a perfect God who doesn't exist, then he could conceive of someone greater than God, which is, of course, impossible.

Therefore God exists.

Because the concept of God is universal, that is all men believe in some kind of god, then God must have placed that idea within man. 'Make sense?

The Atheist

Of course, while we may know of God in our heart, many others don't believe in the existence of God.

All "atheists" deny God.
> The "practical atheist" lives as though there is no God.
> The "dogmatic atheist" openly repudiates God and
> the "virtual atheist" rejects God by his terminology.

The "agnostic" is one who says we can't prove that God even exists, but, different than atheists, agnostics vary in their degrees of skepticism. The agnostic believes that something has to be scientifically provable to warrant belief. It's easy to sense that some agnostics believe in the existence of God, but are too lazy to prove or disprove Him, so they choose to be non-committal. These are the ones who, too often, wake up too late!

The "heretic" is one who may have once believed, but now explicitly denounces God. An heretic is distinct from both an "apostate," who is one who rejects Christ but was formerly a Christian, and a blasphemer, one who insults or shows lack of reverence for God.

"Evolutionists" seek to explain life apart from any involvement of God. Therefore, if God didn't create man, then there is no need for morality because a person would be a merely physical being. How awful to go through life like that!

"Polytheists" believe in many gods.

"Pantheists" believe that everything is God and God is everything.

"Deists" believe that there is no personal God to whom man can relate.

The study of Theology Proper supports a belief in God, not by defining others' arguments for His existence or through rejecting the theories of those who don't believe in Him, but by reinforcing one's belief in God which comes from faith. As we discussed earlier, faith grows proportionally to the number of times one can recall God acting in his or her life.

I once decided to do a 10K run in Louisville. While everyone was milling around before the race, I spotted a young Lieutenant with whom I was serving in the Kentucky National Guard. We decided to step off together when the race started. Before it did, I explained to him that I was not a very fast runner, and if he was interested in going for a "PB (personal best)," then he should go for it. I'd see him again at the finish line.

Eighty percent of life is showing up!

I remember what he said to me. "Hey, Major, you and I are the only ones here from the unit. It don't matter what your time is. Eighty percent of life is showing up!"

What a compliment!

Faith is like that. The fun's really in experiencing it!

God's Revelation

God reveals to us truths about ourselves that we would otherwise never know. Psalms 19:1-6 reveals God in the universe and nature. God has also revealed Himself to all humanity through His providential provision and control (Matthew 5:45, Acts 14:15-17), so that we can and should respond to the grace of God. God reveals Himself through our conscience and our innate consciousness of God (Romans 2:14-15). The little cartoon angel on one shoulder who debates the little cartoon devil on the other shoulder is us, exhibiting our innate consciousness of God.

"Special Revelation" are revealings of special occasions to or through certain people. In the Old Testament were "theophanies" or visible or audible manifestations of God. The greater emphasis of special revelation is through the Holy Spirit and Jesus Christ, such as the Spirit-led writing of Scriptures and the teachings of Jesus. The infallible record also reveals Jesus, and in turn Jesus reveals the Father.

Could it be that God is helping me write this even now, and that somehow, between the lines, God is talking to you, the reader, not so much about what I'm saying, but what God wants you to hear? That would be a special revelation from God to you. And, the answer to my prayers. That would be very good!

The Attributes of God

God is an invisible, personal, living Spirit, distinguished from all other spirits by several kinds of attributes. God is self-existent, eternal and unchanging.

>Intellectually, God is omniscient, faithful and wise.

>Ethically, God is just, merciful and loving.

>Emotionally, God is long suffering and compassionate and detests evil.

>Existentially, God is free, authentic and omnipotent.

Relationally, God is transcendent. He goes beyond ordinary limits. Isaiah 55:8 tells us God's His ways are not our ways. He's way more, in ways we can't know here on Earth. We can't always figure out God, and that's OK, as long as we know He loves us and seeks the best for us, and we trust Him.

God is a spirit. He does not have a body (John 4:24). God is ever present, everywhere. God is the source of all life. He's our source.

God is self-existent. He declares, *"I am that I am* (Exodus 3:14)." John 5:26 says, *"the Father has life in Himself."* God doesn't depend on any other.

God is immutable. He is devoid of all change, and that includes all of his promises to you and me. God's absolutely perfect.

God is one. None other can share His glory (I John 5:21). We glorify Him.

God is Truth. He's perfectly reliable in His revelation and sees all things as they really are. He can be trusted. He's the beginning of all knowledge and makes Himself available to us in order that we might have a fellowship with him. He's the source of all truth, not only in the sphere of morals and religion, but also in every field of scientific endeavor.[2]

God is love. In this is love, not that I loved God, but that He loved me and sent His son to be the propitiation for our sins (John 4:8).

God is *agape* love, that is a love that is reasoned out, rather than a love that is based on simply emotions. God loves me irrespective of my worth or of my returned love. God loves me unconditionally. Is that incredible or what?

God is goodness. God is essentially, absolutely and consummately good.[3]

God is holy. The holiness of God pervades all the other attributes of God and is consistent with all He is and does. He's high and exalted. He's separate from evil and sin.

God cannot not abide where sin exists.

God is eternal. He's not limited in time (Psalms 90:2).

God is immense. He's that perfection of the Divine Being by which He transcends all spatial limitations and yet is present in every point of space with His whole being.[4]

God is omnipresent. He's everywhere present.

God is omniscient. God has all knowledge. He knows all things that exist in actuality. He knows all things that have not yet occurred.

He knows all future events. God's knowledge is intuitive, that is, it is immediate, simultaneous, actual, complete and real.

God in omnipotent. He's all-powerful. Still, God can't do things that are not in harmony with His nature. He can't go back on His word. His promises are true and everlasting. He can't lie and He can't relate to sin. God cannot not abide where sin exists.

God is merciful. God shows me mercy, goodness and love when we are in misery or distress, irrespective of what we may deserve.

God is gracious. He gives unmerited favor to us even when we are under condemnation. He delivers us from enemies, enables us, forgives us and preserves us. God saves us.

God is just. He's entirely correct and just in all His dealings with us.

The Decrees of God

The decrees of God have very practical ramifications:

- We can stand in awe of a great God who is wise, powerful and loving.
- We can trust our entire life to God who is almighty.
- We can rejoice in the wonder of our salvation, that we are the choice of God in eternity past.
- We can rest in peace as we observe a tumultuous world, knowing that God is sovereign over all things.
- God holds us accountable for our sin, but forgives us when we confess.
- We are humbled in His presence and His presence mitigates our pride.

Summary

There's "one and only one" living and true God. He's an intelligent, spiritual, and personal Being, the Creator, Redeemer, Preserver and

Ruler of the universe. God is infinite in holiness and all other perfections. God's all powerful and all knowing and His perfect knowledge extends to all things, past, present and future, including the future decisions of His free creatures.

The eternal triune God reveals Himself to us as Father, Son, and Holy Spirit, with distinct personal attributes, but without division of nature, essence or being.

God as Father reigns with providential care over His universe, His creatures and the flow of the stream of human history according to the purposes of His grace. He's all powerful, all knowing, all loving and all wise. God is Father in truth to those who become children of God through faith in Jesus Christ.[5]

He tells us that if we, as His son or daughter, will humble ourselves and pray and seek His face, and turn from our wicked ways, He'll hear our prayers in Heaven, He'll forgive our sins and trespasses and He'll heal our situations. He's our God and we are His. Praise God!

In her hit song, *"There Will Come A Day,"* country star Faith Hill sings:

> *"It's not easy trying to understand*
> *How the world can be so cold, stealing the souls of man*
> *Cloudy skies rain down on all your dreams*
> *You wrestle with the fear and doubt*
> *Sometimes it's hard but you gotta believe.*
> *There's a better place, where our Father waits*
> *And every tear He'll wipe away*
> *The darkness will be gone, the weak shall be strong*
> *Hold on to your faith*
> *There will come a day, there will come a day*
> *Wars are raging, lives are scattered*
> *Innocence is lost, and hopes are shattered*
> *The old are forgotten, the children are forsaken*
>
> *In this world we're living in*
> *Is there anything sacred?*
> *There will come a day, there will come a day*

The song will ring out, down those golden streets
The voices of Earth with the angels will sing
Every knee will bow, sin will have no trace
In the glory of His amazing grace
Every knee will bow, sin will have no trace
In the glory of His amazing grace
There will come a day, there will come a day."

---

[1] Packer, J. I., *Knowing God* (Downers Grove, IL: , InterVarsity Press, 1973), pp. 14-15.

[2] Berkhof, Lewis, *Systematic Theology* (Grand Rapids: Eerdmans, 1941), pg. 58.

[3] Vine, W. E., *An Expository Dictionary of New Testament Words* (Westwood, NJ: Revell, 1940), 2:163.

[4] Berkhof, *Systematic Theology*, pg. 73.

[5] *Baptist Faith And Message,* a summary of the faith of Southern Baptists, adopted at the Southern Baptist Convention on June 14, 2000. The late Dr. Adrian Rogers, a precious friend of mine, was Chairman of the Committee.

VIII. Walk with the Triune God

Trinitarianism - The Trinity: Father, Son and Holy Ghost

Preface

How can God be the Father and Jesus and the Holy Spirit, too?

Trinitarianism is the belief in, or doctrine of, the Trinity or Triune (*"tri,"* meaning three, *"une"* meaning one, or unity of one) existence of God. Three in One. God is one essence in three Persons.

Understanding the Trinity is not just a conversation starter for pastors and theologians, it's really important for the average Christian. Because, you see, the Trinity is the display of God in all that He did, all He does and all He will do, for us.

The Trinity shows that God is not just a remote "Man upstairs" who built everything and left it up to us to make meaning of it all. Nope. Just the opposite. In the Trinity, we see God as very active in our lives. That's the Plan. And, it's what He wants it to be.

The Oxford Dictionary of the Christian Church describes the Trinity as "the central dogma of Christian theology."[1] Fancy words, but right on.

There are more than sixty Bible verses that likewise mention

> *The Trinity is the display of God in all that He did, all that He does, and all that He will do, for us.*

the three Persons together. The most quoted, perhaps, is Matthew 3:16, the wonderful scene of Jesus before John the Baptist in the Sea of Galilee. *"And Jesus, when He was baptized...saw the Spirit of God descending like a dove and lighting on Him: And lo, a Voice from Heaven saying, 'This is my beloved Son in Whom I am well pleased.'"*

There is only one God, and that God is three Persons:
> God the Father in the voice,
> God the Son in the man, and
> God the Holy Spirit in the dove.

The Father is not the Son. The Son is not the Holy Spirit. The Holy Spirit is not the Father. The Father, Son and Holy Spirit are all God, but they aren't three names for the same person. To an unbeliever or a Muslim, this is confusing, but to a born-again believer like me, who has witnessed all Three Persons acting in his life, it's not confusing at all. We understand the Trinity through our faith. Mostly, because we've seen Him in action.

God is one absolutely perfect divine Being, in three Persons. The three essences of God are called Persons because they relate to each other in very Person-al ways. Understand?

Of the Father, the Son and the Holy Spirit, the Father is God.
> He is the First Person of the Trinity.

The Son is God.
> He is the Second Person of the Trinity.

And, the Holy Spirit, also called the Holy Ghost, is God.
> He is the Third Person of the Trinity.

The Bible teaches that there is only one God, yet all three Persons are called God.

The Bible Tells of the Triune God

First, one must understand that there is only one God. Moses tells us clearly in Deuteronomy 6:4, to *"Hear, O Israel. The Lord our God is one Lord."* God Himself tells us through his prophet Isaiah that, *"Before me [God] there was no God formed, neither shall there be [any God] after me (Isaiah 43:10b)."*

The Father is God. Paul addresses us in I Corinthians 8:6, *"Grace unto you, and peace, from God our Father..."* And again in Ephesians 4:4-6, referring to *"...one God and Father of all."*

The Son is God. The apostle John clearly identifies the Son as God in John 1:1, especially when read in context with John 1:14: *In the beginning was the Word, and the Word was with God and the Word was God....And the Word was made flesh and dwelt among us."* Through the rest of the Scriptures in the first chapter of the Book of John, the apostle clearly paints a picture of the activities of the Trinity in the formulation of the world, as the Creator and as the Sustainer of all believers.

God the Son, Jesus, identifies Himself as one with God the Father, when He says, *"I and the Father are one (John 10:30-33)."*

The apostle Thomas addressed Jesus as, both *"My Lord and my God"* in John 20:28.

Many Bible passages clearly declare that Jesus Christ is Lord and God of both the New Testament and the Old Testament. Jesus is God.

The Holy Spirit is God. When Ananias withheld his offerings to God, the apostle Peter admonished him and asked why Satan had filled his heart *"to lie to the Holy Ghost?"* (Acts 5:3). Clearly, Peter identified the Holy Ghost as God.

In his second letter to the Corinthians, the apostle Paul identifies that *"the Lord is that Spirit"* (II Corinthians 3:17). We can also see in these passages that this declaration is made amidst a teaching of the fullness of revelation in Christ, thereby once again offering a comprehensive illustration of the Trinity at work: God the Father, God the Son and God the Holy Ghost.

Jesus commanded us in the Great Commandment of Matthew 28:19, to *"teach all nations and baptize them in the name of the Father, and of the Son, and of the Holy Ghost."* In this passage, Jesus doesn't identify Himself as the Father, Son and Holy Ghost. He is saying that Christian baptism identifies a person as one who *believes* in the Father, in the Son whom the Father sent to die for our sins, and in the Holy Spirit whom the Father and the Son send to dwell in the heart of Christians like you and me.

The apostle Paul gives us another picture of the Persons of God when he commends us in II Corinthians 13:14 with the grace of God the Son, the love of God the Father and the communion of God the Holy Spirit.

The word "Trinity" is not in the Bible, but the Works of Him are everywhere.

The apostle Peter gives a similar greeting in I Peter 1:2, citing the blood of Jesus, the foreknowledge of the Father and the sanctification of the Holy Spirit, multiplied into a single grace and peace.

"Trinity" in the Bible

The word "trinity" does not appear in the Bible, but the Trinity is very much a Biblical belief, and the examples of the Trinity, or Triune God are everywhere. Without actually using the word, many Bible passages define the Trinity as the eternal relationship between the Father, the Son and the Holy Ghost.

Besides the overwhelming evidence in Bible Scriptures, early church leaders like Clement and Ignatius wrote of the Trinity, and they did so even before some of the New Testament was written, and less than a mere seventy years after Jesus' death.

And, according to Irish legend, Saint Patrick, in about 432 AD, explained the Trinity with the visual aid of a shamrock. Whether or not the legend is true, the illustration is excellent:

"Is this one leaf or three?" he asked. *"If one leaf, why are there three lobes of equal size? If three leaves, why is there only one stem? If mankind cannot explain so simple a mystery as a shamrock, than how can he hope to understand one so profound as the Holy Trinity* [to which I must add, "without faith"]*?"* God the Father, God the Son and God the Holy Ghost.

One final illustration is that of water. It can be found in ice, steam and the liquid, yet all have the same nature, water. Unlike water, however, the wonder of the Trinity is that the Father, Son and Holy Spirit are all God at the same time.

The Work of God and Jesus Compared

The first verse of the Bible tells us that *"In the beginning God created the heaven and the earth* (Genesis 1:1)," and in Psalms 102, David cries to *"my God..."* that the *"heavens are the work of thy* [God's] *hands."* John tells us in the first chapter of his Book that all things are created in and through Jesus, *"the Word"* (John 1:3).

This is not a contradiction. It's the same God.

Same God. Two Persons.

Isaiah (Isaiah 44:6) calls God, *"the first and the last,"* and the Revelation of St. John the Divine attributes the very same title to Jesus, *"the first and the last,"* (Revelation 1:17, and 22:13).

David calls God the *"Judge of all people"* in Psalms 94:2. John, Luke and Paul all call Jesus the same *"Judge of all people"* in John 5:22, Acts 17:31 and II Corinthians 5:10.

Same God. Two Persons. God and Jesus.

God Himself tells us in Jeremiah 33:3 that He hears and answers the prayers of all who call on Him. Jesus Himself tells us that He, too, hears and answers prayer of those who call on Him, in John 14:14.

Same God. Two Persons. God and Jesus.

Jesus forgives sin, stakes His claim to be the divine Son of God, and accepts worship as God on the same level of power and honor as the Father in Matthew 28:18. That's because Jesus is co-equal with God.

Jesus is God.

The Work of God the Holy Spirit and Jesus Compared

Jesus willingly spent His life on Earth and gave it up that we might know the Father and witness the power and love of the Holy Spirit. John, in chapter 17, tells us that when Jesus rose from that grave, He ascended to Heaven and returned to the glory of the Father, His glory, that same glory as defined in both in the Old Testament in Isaiah 42:8, and in the New Testament in John 17:5. Jesus told His disciples and us that He would never leave us alone, but that He would always reside with us in the Person of the Holy Spirit, and as such He will teach us all things and bring all things to our remembrance whatsoever He said unto us (John 14:16 and 26).

    Same God. Two Persons. Jesus and the Holy Spirit.

Like the other Persons of the Trinity, the Holy Spirit is eternal (Hebrews 9:14), omnipresent (Psalms 139:7) and omniscient (I Corinthians 2:10) and wills and acts supernaturally (I Corinthians 12:11). He is called the Creator of all things in Psalms 104:30.

Like the other Persons of the Trinity, the Holy Spirit is a giver of life in Romans 8:10 and in John 3:8. And, Paul teaches us that the Holy Spirit strengthens believers like you and me, in Ephesians 3:16. Every born-again believer knows that to be true.

    Same God. Three Persons. God and Jesus and the Holy Spirit.

Summary

The most profound concept that God teaches, over and over again, to Abraham, Isaac and Jacob and then the people of Israel, is that He is "I Am," He is One alone, and there is no other God. All other gods are false. Period. The first of the Ten Commandments given by God to Israel through the Prophet Moses was to have no other gods before God (Exodus 20:1-6).

God even told us in Isaiah 48:11b, that, *"I will not give my glory to another,"* and especially to *"Harken unto me O Jacob and Israel, my called; I am He; I am the first, I also am the last* (Isaiah 48:12)."

Yet, throughout the Holy Word, we're called to worship God in the Persons of the Holy Spirit and the Messiah, Jesus Christ. How do we worship the Holy Spirit? The same way we worship the Father and the Son.

Worship flows from the inward workings of the Holy Spirit to which we respond by offering our lives to Him (Romans 12:1). We worship the Spirit by obedience to His commands. Referring to Christ, the Apostle John explains that *"those who obey his commands live in him, and he in them. And this is how we know that he lives in us: We know it by the Spirit he gave us"* (I John 3:24). Notice the link between obeying Christ and the Holy Spirit who dwells within us, convicting us of all things, especially our need to worship by obedience, and empowering us to worship.

Worship is itself a function of the Spirit. Jesus says that we *"worship in spirit and in truth"* (John 4:24). His presence in our hearts enables us to return worship to Him in the Spirit. We are in Him as He is in us, just as Christ is in the Father and the Father is in us through the Spirit (John 14:20, 17:21).

There's one God, God the Father, God the Son and God the Holy Ghost.

There are many Bible Scriptures that attest to the Work of the Trinity:

The Trinity is God:
    Father: II Timothy 1:2
    Son: Hebrews 1:8; Philippians 2:11; John 1:1, 18
    Holy Spirit: Acts 5:3-4, Isaiah 40:13-18

The Trinity is Creator:
    Father: Isaiah 64:8
    Son: John 1:1-3, Col 1:15-16, Hebrews 1:3
    Holy Spirit: Job 33:4, 26:13

The Trinity is all-knowing:
    Father: I John 3:20
    Son: John 16:30
    Holy Spirit: I Corinthians 2:10-11

The Trinity is everywhere:
    Father: I Kings 8:27
    Son: Matthew 28:20
    Holy Spirit: Psalms 139:7

The Trinity speaks:
    Father: Matthew 3:17
    Son: Luke 5:20; 7:48
    Holy Spirit: Acts 8:29; 11:12; 13:2

The Trinity loves:
    Father: John 3:16
    Son: Ephesians 5:25
    Holy Spirit: Romans 15:30

The Trinity judges:
    Father: John 5:30, 12:48-50
    Son: John 5:22-23, 30
    Holy Spirit: John 16:7-11

The Trinity is our Savior:
    Father: Isaiah 43:10-11; I Timothy 1:1; 2:3; 4:10
    Son: Matthew 1:21-23, Luke 9:56, John 3:17, Titus 1:4; 3:6
    Holy Spirit: Romans 8:9, I John 4:13, Ephesians 1:13-14

The Trinity gives life:
    Father: Genesis 2:7
    Son: John 1:3, 5:21
    Holy Spirit: John 6:63, II Corinthians 3:6

The Trinity gives joy:
    Father: Psalms 16:11
    Son: John 15:11
    Holy Spirit: Romans 14:7, Galatians 5:22

The Trinity resurrects:
    Father: I Thessalonians 1:10
    Son: John 6:44, 11:25-26
    Holy Spirit: Romans 8:11

Walk with the Triune God

The Trinity indwells believers:
    Father: II Corinthians 6:16, Ephesians 4:6, I John 2:23, II John 1:9
    Son: Revelation 3:20, Colossians 1:27, II Corinthians 13:5
    Holy Spirit: John 14:17, I Corinthians 6:19

The Trinity sanctifies:
    Father: I Thessalonians 5:23
    Son: I Corinthians 1:30, Hebrews 2:11, 10:10
    Holy Spirit: I Peter 1:2

The Trinity searches the heart:
    Father: Jeremiah 17:10
    Son: Revelation 2:23
    Holy Spirit: I Corinthians 2:10

We belong to the Trinity:
    Father: Psalms 24:1
    Son: John 17:6
    Holy Spirit: I Corinthians 6:19-20

We believe in the Trinity:
    Father: John 14:1
    Son: John 14:1
    Holy Spirit: Matthew 12:31-32, Hebrews 3:7-8

We serve the Trinity:
    Father: Matthew 4:10
    Son: Colossians 3:24
    Holy Spirit: John 6:63, Romans 8:14

The Benediction, with the Trinity:
    II Corinthians 13:14: *"The grace of the Lord Jesus Christ, and the love of God, and the fellowship of the Holy Spirit, be with you all."*

Jesus' Commandment with the Trinity:

Matthew 28:18-20: *"And Jesus came up and spoke to them, saying, 'All authority has been given to Me in Heaven and on Earth. Go therefore and make disciples of all the nations, baptizing them in the name of the Father and the Son and the Holy Spirit, teaching them to observe all that I commanded you, and lo, I am with you always, even to the end of the age.'"*

So, the Trinity is the Triune God. He creates. He resurrects. He is everywhere. He indwells believers like you and me. He's all-knowing, He sanctifies, gives life, speaks, loves and searches the heart. We belong to the Trinity. He's our Savior, our judge and our joy-giver.

That's why we serve Him.

The Triune God.

---

[1] *The Oxford Dictionary of the Christian Church* (Oxford University Press, 2005), ISBN 978-0-19-280290-3, article entitled *"Doctrine of the Trinity."*

IX. Walk with Angels

Angelology - Angels all around us - Devils, too

Preface

Do angels really exist?

Did you know that a recent survey by the *Pew Forum* found that 68 percent of Americans say they believe in angels?[1] Just a walk through New York's Metropolitan Museum of Art illustrates that the belief in angels exists all around the world. One angel statue there came from a palace in what is now Iraq, built around 850 years before Jesus. Angels are called "God's Secret Agents" in a book by Billy Graham. And even rock musician Carlos Santana claims that since 1994, he's communicated with an angel named Metatron (I'm not makin' this up) who operates as his "inner voice."[2]

Angelology is the branch of theology that is concerned with angels. The Hebrew word for angel is *"malak"* which simply means "messenger." The word may refer to a human messenger as in I Kings 19:2, or a divine messenger or angel as in Genesis 28:12. As a divine messenger, an angel is a *"heavenly being, charged by God with some commission."*[3]

Angels do exist.

Do you believe in angels? You should. Angels do exist. They are good, messengers of God. Many Christians believe that they have been visited by angels many times in their life, although most often while unaware of their presence.

Likewise, Satan is surely real. He's a bad angel and if we're going to talk about angels, we have to include him. He and his bad angels have attacked Christians like me often, likely daily. Yet, through the Blood of Jesus and the Holy Spirit that lives within us, Satan is only as successful as we'll allow Him to be in our imperfect human being.

Praise God, God protects us from Satan and any plan that he or an enemy angel might conjure against us.

Through the Blood of Jesus and the Holy Spirit that lives within me, Satan is only as successful as I'll allow Him to be.

I've never audibly heard the voice of an angel, but I sure have felt a heavenly presence and I wouldn't discount that such could be the presence of angels sent to minister to me.

The Hebrew word for angel, *"malak,"* is found 103 times in the Old Testament. The Greek word with a similar meaning, *"angelos,"* from which we get our word "angels," is found 175 times in the New Testament. It also means *"messenger... who speaks and acts in the place of the one who has sent him."*[4]

Mathematically, that's four mentions of angels, on average, for every book in the Bible. Angels are a big part of the Word!

Angels are called *"sons of God* (small 's')*"* because, in their unfallen state, they are God's sons by His creation (Job 1:6, 38:7). They are also called *"holy ones"* because they are set apart by God and for God to be attendants to His Holiness. Together, they are sometimes called the *"host"* or *"host of heaven"* as a picture of the armies of Heaven (Psalms 89:6 and I Samuel 17:45). Theology holds that multiplied numbers of angels surround God in Heaven, from which we get one of the names of God, as the *"Lord of Hosts* (Isaiah 31:4)*."*

Angels and Us

A better understanding of angels is fortified by comparing them to humans:

All angels were created before or during the formation of the earth according to Job 38:4-7. Since angels were created, they were created by God. Therefore, they were created as holy beings, since a holy God could create no other.[5]

Humans, of course, were created with Adam and Eve after the earth was formed. That is our lineage as a human.

Angels are spiritual beings, compared to wind and flame in Psalms 104:4 and Hebrews 1:7, but they are capable of taking on a physical form (Genesis 18:2-8 and 19:1-3).

Humans like us have a physical body with a spiritual side that goes beyond the physical (Genesis 3:19, Psalms 42:2, Matthew 10:28 and II Corinthians 4:16). The misunderstanding of one's spiritual side is an unfortunate and major reason why many don't seek to receive Christ as Savior. It's also one reason this book was written, and hopefully, one of the reasons you're reading it now!

Angels live in Heaven, but they can visit earth (Matthew 18:10).

Humans live on Earth but they can go to Heaven (Luke 23:43, II Corinthians 12:1-4), which we surely will as born-again believers.

Angels are not reinvented human beings, as the Mormons claim in their belief of the angel Moroni who supposedly visited Joseph Smith, or as the Mormon belief and doctrine that we shall be resurrected as angels having bodies of flesh and bones.[6]

Our ascension to Heaven will be much better than that.

Angels are God's created sons (Job 1:6, Psalms 89:6).

Humans are God's adopted sons (Romans 8:14-23, Galatians 3:26, 4:4-6).

Isn't it fun to say, *"I'm an adopted son of God"* (John 1:12)?

If angels sin, they can't be redeemed (Hebrews 2:14-17), but

if humans sin, they can be redeemed by trusting in Jesus and the sacrificial shedding if His blood on the cross of Calvary (Hebrews 2:14-17).

"I am redeemed, praise God!" That's fun to say, too!

God's holy angels will live forever with God. Satan and his fallen angels will be punished and banned from God's presence forever.

Humans who are made right with God, as you and I have been by the Blood of Jesus, will live forever with God as the angels will. Everyone else will be banished from God's presence (Matthew 25:46, Revelation 20:10-15) to an eternal hell.

> *There is rejoicing in the presence of angels of God over one sinner who repents."*
> *Hebrews 1:16*

I love the fact that angels have some sort of kinship with me. The Bible says, *"There is rejoicing in the presence of angels of God over one sinner who repents"* (Hebrews 1:16).

First, angels rejoiced over me. Isn't that a wonderful thought!

Second, that's the same feeling I get when one repents in my presence, so I can only assume that angels are in at least some ways, just like me.

Demons

Unfortunately, not all angels or spiritual beings are on God's side. There are an undetermined number of demons who are Satan's fallen angels (Matthew 25:41). Satan himself disguises himself as an *"angel of light"* in II Corinthians 11:14, therefore, one must be cautious and compare all influences to Scripture to be certain of purity and truth (Matthew 22:19, Acts 17:11, II Timothy 3:16). God's angels will not contradict the Bible. Satan's will.

The angel Lucifer, originally placed in authority over all the angels, is the one who fell from Heaven (Isaiah 14:12) after a series of *"I will..."* declarations and became Satan our adversary. Give Satan an inch & he'll be a ruler. So, never give the devil a ride - he'll always want to drive. That's not God's Plan.

How Do We Know That Angels Exist?

First, the Scriptures tell about angels. Thirty-four of the Bible's sixty-six books make reference to angels.

Second, Jesus tells us about angels: Angels helped Him following His temptation (Matthew 4:11). Jesus Himself referred to His resurrected state as being comparable to that of angels (Matthew 22:29-30) and Jesus taught that angels will gather the nation of Israel at the time of His return (Matthew 25:31-32, 41).

The Nature and Ministry of Angels

Angels are spiritual beings says Hebrews 1:14. They don't marry and they don't die. They're created beings, being created at the beginning of time, but they're not being created anymore. While we humans are made *"a little lower than the angels"* (Hebrews 2:7), we shall be exalted above angels at our resurrection and in the consummation of age (I Corinthians 6:3).

Angels have rank. The archangel Michael is of the highest ranking, the protector of Israel. Ruling angels are mentioned in Ephesians 3:10, but just what they rule is uncertain.

The angel Gabriel appears in the Bible record four times, where he reveals and interprets God's purpose and program concerning Messiah and His kingdom to the prophets and people of Israel. Muslims believe that Allah revealed the Qur'an to Muhammad through the angel Gabriel, the Qur'an being the fundamental source of Islam.

The Bible tells us for certain in Daniel 8:1-6, that Gabriel is the angel who explained to Daniel the succeeding kingdoms of Medo-Persia and Greece as well as the untimely death of Alexander the Great. He announced the birth of John the Baptist to Zachariah in Luke 1:11-20. In his most well-known act, Gabriel was the angel who told Mary of Jesus, His birth and ministry.

Angels Minister to God

The cherubim is the angel band that surrounds the throne of God. Cherubs fiercely guard the Tree of Life (Genesis 3:24), the Arc of the Covenant, the Temple of God (II Chronicles 5:7-8) and the Heavenly Throne Room (Revelation 4:6-9). Cool job, huh?

The seraphim are angels who also guard the Throne Room. They cry, *"Holy, holy, holy,"* praising and proclaiming the perfect holiness of God, and they declare that man must be sinless to stand in God's presence.

Angels Minister to Christ

We know that angels work as messengers of God. Colossians 1:16 indicates that angels were also created by Jesus to give praise to Him. And, we know from Scripture, that angels ministered to Jesus throughout his earthly reign:

Angels predicted His birth.

Angels protected Him as a baby, warning Joseph to flee to Egypt from Herod.

Angels gave Him food and encouragement after His temptation.

Angels strengthened Him at Gethsemane as He wrestled with His upcoming crucifixion (Matthew 26:52).

Angels announced His resurrection to the women at His tomb.

Angels attended His ascension, and reminded us of His return.

Angels will prepare us and attend His Second Coming (Matthew 24:31).

"He could have called ten thousand angels
To destroy the world and set Him free.
He could have called ten thousand angels,
But He died alone, for you and me."[7]

Angels Minister to You and Me

Angels have been commissioned and sent to minister to you and me.

Angels frustrate plans of our enemies (Psalms 35:4-5), and they will protect the 144,000 in tribulation (Revelation 7:1-14).

Angels give us physical provision, as they did Elijah when he was weakened from a long journey (I Kings 19:5-7).

Angels give us encouragement (Acts 27:23-25).

Angels give us direction (Acts 8:26).

Angels assist in answers to our prayers. As they did in Peter's release from prison (Acts 12:1-11), they assist in releasing us from the bondages of this world.

Angels will carry us home, *"absent from the body... at home with the Lord"* (II Corinthians 5:8). "Hallelujah! What a day that will be!

Angels will mete out judgment to unbelievers and during the final judgment, the angels will separate the "sons of the evil one" from the "sons of the kingdom." Matthew 13 records Jesus' teaching on the parable of the wheat and the tares. Tares were weeds that grew alongside the wheat and looked just like wheat. But, when one cracked open a husk of a mature plant, there was wheat to harvest, but the tare was empty. There was no meat, no commitment, no value. Jesus said, *"The Son of Man will send his angels. They will gather everything in his kingdom that causes people to sin and everyone who does evil. The angels will throw them into a blazing furnace. People will cry and be in extreme pain there. Then the people who have God's approval will shine like the sun in their Father's kingdom. Let the person who has ears listen!"* (Matthew 13:39-43 GNV).

The Other Side: Satan

In his book, "*The Moody Handbook of Theology*," author Paul Enns says, "*The primary witness to the reality and existence of Satan is not experience or sensational stories, but the testimony of Scripture.*"[8]

While on the surface, that position might be hard to debate, many believe that most of God's children are attacked by the Adversary constantly, perhaps daily or every moment. We just don't realize it, nor are such attacks as open or manifested as extensively as are the Old and New Testament evidence about Satan.

As the serpent in Genesis, Satan ushered in man's original sin. He was Job's accuser and in Zechariah, the accuser of the nation. Every writer in the New Testament refers to him, in a myriad of names including Beelzebub, Belial, Abaddon and Apollyon the Destroyer.

He's also the enemy, tempter, murderer, liar, slanderer, deceiver and accuser. He's the God of the world and the prince of the power of the air. He's the ultimate adversary.

He's a schemer and intelligent (Matthew 4:5-6). He's emotional, too, even to the point of losing his high angelic state in his desire to exalt himself above the rule of God (Isaiah 14:12-14).

Still, Satan doesn't have infinite power. He is still accountable to God as seen in the story of Job. Christ has won victory over Satan for you and me and all others who place their trust in Jesus. In his judgment, Satan not only fell from his exalted position, but his defeat by Christ was ultimate and he was rendered powerless through the Cross. The Bible says he will be cast out of Heaven during the tribulation (Revelation 12:13), bound in the pit for a thousand years (Revelation 20:2-3), and finally be cast in the lake of fire for eternity (Revelation 20:7-10).

So much for Satan.

Demons Who Attack Us

In short, demons are deceivers who are angels of Satan. Some are confined to Hell, apparently too depraved and harmful to be allowed to roam upon the earth.[9] Other demons are free and active in the world today. Demons, or fallen angels, also have rank, some of them rank highly on Earth.

> *Every time Satan reminds you of your past, you just remind Satan of his future!*

Although they exist to harass God's children, demons can't be omnipresent and they are aware of their destiny. So, every time they remind you of your past, just remind them of their future!

Demons are spirit beings. Demons are powerful but not omnipotent, witness the man of the Gerasenes who could break the chains of his shackles by his enormous strength (Mark 5:3-4). A demon sought to have a boy commit suicide by throwing him into fire and water (Mark 9:22). A demon possession debilitated a man's speech (Matthew 9:32) and kept a girl in cruel slavery (Matthew 15:22). Yet, demons are limited in their power (John 10:21).

Demons inflict disease (Luke 13:11), influence the mind (Genesis 3:1-5), and deceive people (I Thessalonians 3:5), and nations.

Demons will eventually gather the nations of the world together in rebellion against Christ. Some say this is already happening in our world today. Revelations 16:14 tells us that demons will deceive the world by performing signs in order to incite warfare against the returning Messiah. This may be why Pope Benedict XVI recently called attention to the plight of Christians who are targeted in Islamic violence during his Mideast visit. The Pope called for international support to ensure the survival of the ancient Christian community there.[10]

Charles Ryrie, in his study graph of *Bible Doctrine II*, defines demon possession as, *"A demon residing in a person, exerting direct control and influence over that person, with certain derangement of mind and/ or body. Demon possession is to be distinguished from demon influence or demon activity in relation to a person. The work of the demon in the latter is from the outside; in demon possession it is from within."*[11]

> *Demons can't possess a born-again Christian.*

Demons can't possess a born-again Christian. That's because we are indwelt by the Person of the Holy Spirit. *"Greater is He that is within me than he that is in the world"* (I John 4:4).

Summary

Angels minister to us constantly, more than we know. As in Hebrews 1:14, angels bring us messages of how to live our lives for Christ. The "still small voice" we hear inaudibly is often that of angels.

Hebrews 13:2 tells us that we should show hospitality to strangers, as we might be hosting angels unaware. I believe that. Most of us try to be hospitable, because that's what Christ would have us do. Angels are wonderful, but they are messengers, not friends.

No one should be afraid of demons or of Satan. Their power is limited, and no match for that of Christ our Victor. Through Him, we are saved, and protected from any demonic possession.

So the problem for people today is not simply believing that angels exist, but in their ability to distinguish between angels and demons.[12] The Bible says, *"He will give his angels charge over you in all your ways"* (Psalms 91:11). And, you and I can believe that.

What a Friend we have in Jesus!

Let's take a break, and let me tell you about <u>Santa and Sarah and the Angels</u>:

Some time ago, a little boy and his grandmother came to see Santa at the mall. The boy climbed up on Santa's lap, holding a picture of a little girl.

"Who's this?" asked Santa, smiling. "Your friend?

"Yes, Santa," he replied. "My sister, Sarah, who's very sick," he said sadly. Santa glanced over at the grandmother who was waiting nearby, and saw her dabbing her eyes with a tissue.

"Sarah wanted to come with me to see you, oh, so very much, Santa!" the child exclaimed. "She misses you," he added softly.

Santa tried to be cheerful and encouraged a smile to the boy's face, asking him what he wanted Santa to bring him for Christmas. When they finished their visit, the grandmother came over to help the child off his lap, and started to say something to Santa, but halted.

"What is it?" Santa asked warmly.

"Well, I know it's really too much to ask you, Santa, but...." the old woman began, shooing her grandson over to one of Santa's elves to collect the little gift which Santa gave all his young visitors. "The girl in the photograph... my granddaughter... well, you see she has leukemia and isn't expected to make it even through the holidays," she said through tear-filled eyes. "Is there any way, Santa, any possible way that you could come see Sarah? That's all she's asked for, for Christmas, is to see Santa."

Santa blinked and swallowed hard and told the woman to leave information with his elves as to where Sarah was, and he would see what he could do. Santa thought of little else the rest of that afternoon. He knew what he had to do. "What if it were MY child lying in that hospital bed, dying," he thought with a sinking heart, "This is the least I can do."

When Santa finished is work that evening, he retrieved from his helper, Rick, the name of the hospital where Sarah was staying. He asked how to get to the hospital.

"Why?" Rick asked, with a puzzled look on his face. Santa relayed to him the conversation with Sarah's grandmother earlier that day.

"C'mon, I'll take you there." Rick said. Rick drove them to the hospital and came inside with Santa.

They found out which room Sarah was in. A pale Rick said he'd wait out in the hall.

Santa quietly peeked into the room through the half-closed door and saw little Sarah in the bed.

The room was full of what appeared to be her family; there was the grandmother and the girl's brother he'd met earlier that day. A woman whom he guessed was Sarah's mother stood by the bed, gently pushing Sarah's thin hair off her forehead. Another woman who he discovered later was Sarah's aunt, sat in a chair near the bed with a weary sad look on her face. They were talking quietly, and Santa could sense the warmth and closeness of the family, and their love and concern for Sarah.

Taking a deep breath, and forcing a smile on his face, Santa entered the room, bellowing a hearty, "Ho, Ho, Ho!"

"Santa!" shrieked little Sarah, weakly as she tried to escape her bed to run to him, IV tubes intact.

Santa rushed to her side and gave her a warm hug. She was a child about the tender age of his own son - 9 years old. Excitedly, she gazed up at him with wonder and excitement. Her skin was pale and her short tresses bore telltale bald patches from the effects of chemotherapy. But, all he saw when he looked at her was a pair of huge blue eyes. His heart melted, and he had to force himself to choke back tears. Though his eyes were riveted upon Sarah's face, he could hear the gasps and quiet sobbing of the women in the room.

As he and Sarah began talking, the family crept quietly to the bedside one by one, squeezing Santa's shoulder or his hand gratefully, whispering "Thank you" as they gazed sincerely at him with shining eyes. Santa and Sarah talked and talked, and she told him excitedly all the toys she wanted for Christmas, assuring him she'd been a very good girl that year.

As their time together dwindled, Santa felt led in his spirit to pray for Sarah, and asked for permission from the girl's mother. She nodded in agreement and the entire family circled around Sarah's bed, holding hands. Santa looked intensely at Sarah and asked her if she believed in angels.

"Oh, yes, Santa... I do!" she exclaimed.

"Well, I'm going to ask God to send angels to watch over you." he said. Then, laying one hand on the child's head, Santa closed his eyes and prayed. He asked God to touch little Sarah and heal her body from this disease. He asked that angels minister to her, watch and keep her.

And when he finished praying, still with eyes closed, he started singing, softly, *"Silent Night, Holy Night....all is calm, all is bright..."* The family joined in, still holding hands, smiling at Sarah, and crying tears of hope, tears of joy for this moment, as Sarah beamed at them all.

When the song ended, Santa sat on the side of the bed again and held Sarah's frail, small hands in his own. "Now, Sarah," he said authoritatively, "You have a job to do, and that is to concentrate on getting well. I want you to have fun playing with your friends this summer, and I expect to see you at my house at the mall this time next year!"

He knew it was risky proclaiming that to this little girl who had terminal cancer, but he "had" to. He had to give her the greatest gift he could -- not dolls or games or toys -- but the gift of hope.

"OK, Santa!" Sarah exclaimed, her eyes bright.

He leaned down and kissed her on the forehead and left the room. Out in the hall, the minute Santa's eyes met Rick's, a look passed between the two men and they wept unashamed.

Sarah's mother and grandmother slipped out of the room quickly and rushed to Santa's side to thank him.

"My only child is the same age as Sarah," he explained quietly. "This is the least I could do." They nodded with understanding and hugged him.

A year later, Santa was again back on the set in the mall for his six-week, seasonal job which he so loves to do. Several weeks went by and then one day a child came up to sit on his lap.

"Hi, Santa! Remember me?!"

"Of course, I do," Santa proclaimed (as he always does), smiling down at her. After all, the secret to being a "good" Santa is to always make each child feel as if they are the "only" child in the world at that moment.

"You came to see me in the hospital last year!"

Santa's jaw dropped. Tears immediately sprang in his eyes, and he grabbed this little miracle and held her to his chest. "Sarah!" he exclaimed. He scarcely recognized her, for her hair was long and silky and her cheeks were rosy -- much different from the sick little girl he had visited just a year before. He looked over and saw Sarah's mother and grandmother in the sidelines smiling and waving and wiping their eyes.

That was the best Christmas ever for Santa Claus. He had witnessed answered prayer, and this miracle of hope. Sarah was healed. Cancer-free. Alive and well. He silently looked up to Heaven and humbly whispered, "Thank you, Father. 'Tis a very, Merry Christmas, indeed!"

Do you believe in God? Do you believe in angels?

Santa and Sarah sure do.

"In a world full of trouble we travel along.
God is our Father, we're on our way home.
If forces of evil ever close in on you,
Jesus has promised, this is what He will do.
(He'll) Put angels all around you, to keep you from harm,
To guide and direct you, 'till you're safe in His arms.
With angels all around you, you're never alone
And you'll be protected 'till you make it home.
The prophet Elijah, in the Bible we're told
Approached by an army just stood there so bold.
Cause he heard God's whisper "Fear not my son,
Just look toward the Heavens, see what I have done." [4]

---

[1] Pew Forum on Religion & Public Life, Washington, DC, 2008.

[2] Chris Heath, "The Epic Life of Carlos Santana," *Rolling Stone,* March 2000.

[3] van Rad, Gerhard, *"Mal'ak* in the Old Testament," in Gerhard Kittel, ed., *Theological Dictionary of the New Testament,* 10 vols., (Grand Rapids, Eerdmans, 1964), 1:76-77.

[4] Beitenhard, H., "Angel," in Colin Brown, ed., *New International Dictionary of New Testament Theology,* 4 vols. (Grand Rapids: Zondervan, 1975), 1:101.

[5] Hobbs, Hershel H., *What Baptists Believe* (Nashville: Broadman Press, 1964), "Angels," pg. 125.

[6] lds.about.com, Latter-Day Saints

[7] Overholt, Ray., writer of the song, *Ten Thousand Angels,* sung by Loretta Lynn and others. Overholt was playing nightclubs when he realized he needed to quit the drinking, smoking bar lifestyle. Overholt wasn't a Christian but he knew people were praying for him, and while he'd written many songs, he'd never written one about Jesus. So, he opened the Bible and started reading about Christ in the garden of Gethsemane. *I read where Jesus told Peter that he could ask his Father and he would send twelve legions of angels,"* he told SoGospelNews.com. *"I didn't know at the time that that would have been more than 72,000 angels. I knew I needed Christ,"* Overbold said, *"so I knelt there and accepted, as my Savior, the One whom I had been singing and writing about."*

[8] Enns, Paul, *The Moody Handbook of Theology,* (Chicago: Moody Publishers, 2008), pg. 156.

[9] Under, Merrill, F., *Demons in the World Today* (Wheaton, IL: Tyndall, 1971), pg. 16.

[10] Religion Section, *The Dallas Morning News,* Friday, May 15, 2009, pg. 14A.

[11] Ryrie, Charles C., *Study-Graph: Bible Doctrine II* (Chicago: Moody, 1965)

[12] Graham, Billy, *Angels* (Dallas: Word Publishing, 1994), *Preface,* pg. 3.

[13] Hemphill, Joel, *"Angels All Around You,"* 1984. Recorded and Sung by Buddy Merrick & Praise on our album, *"Double Helping of Gospel Country,"* 2000.

X. Walk in Fellowship

Ecclesiology - Fellowship in the Church

Preface

"A lot of church members singing 'Standing on the Promises' are really just sitting on the premises."

Some ask, "Do I have to fellowship with a church to be a Christian?" Well, let's see.

Ecclesiology is the study of the doctrine of the church *(ekklesis)*, both the local church and the universal church, in all its definitions: the body, the bride, the branches, the building, the priesthood and the flock.

Church functions include worshiping, instructing, fellowshipping, sending out missionaries and ministering through elders, deacons and pastors. Churches are governed in different ways, especially in the conduct of ordinances such as the Lord's Supper and Baptism.

> *Forsake not the assembly of one another.*

In addition to its local work, it's the job of the church to minister worldwide, to teach all nations, baptize them in the name of the Trinity, and to comfort others with the omnipresent love of God.

The First Methodist Church had a ministry to the military. One day, when little Johnny came to church, he stopped short in the church lobby, looking up at a plaque on the wall.

"Daddy, what's that?" he asked.

"That's a memorial to all those who died in the service," Dad explained.

"Which service? The nine O'clock service or the eleven O'clock one?" Johnny asked.

It took a while, but Dad finally got Johnny to understand why we fellowship!

The Local Church

"Local church" fellowships of believers met most often in homes, just like your Tuesday night Bible study, or in churches without buildings. Included was the church in Jerusalem (Acts 8:1, 11:22), in Asia Minor (Acts 16:5, in Rome (Romans 16:5), in Corinth (I Corinthians 1:2, II Corinthians 1:1), in Galatia (Galatians 1:2), in Thessalonica (I Thessalonians 1:1) and in the house of Philemon (Philemon 2).

These congregations worked in the same basic ministries, and thanks to their work, people were continually being saved (Acts 2:47).

Much of that can't be said of our churches in America today. That's sad.

The Universal Church

The "universal church" includes all those who, in this Age, have been born again, and by that Spirit have been baptized into the Body of Christ (I Corinthians 12:13, I Peter 1:3, 22-25).[1] This was the corporate group of believers that Christ promised to build in Matthew 16:18, for whom He died in Ephesians 5:25, and for which He is still the head, giving it direction, according to Ephesians 1:22-23 and Colossians 1:18.

A particular emphasis of the

> *"Upon this rock I will build my church; and the gates of hell shall not prevail against it."*
> Jesus in Matthew 16:18

universal church is of course, unity. That's because whether Jew or Gentile, it's inspired by the Holy Spirit. Augustine, Luther and Calvin all referred to the universal church as the "invisible church," while the local congregation was referred to as the "visible body." In their distinction, the invisible church was more pure, not possessing the imperfections of the visible church.[2]

Foundations of the Church

When Jesus told Peter, *"I will build my church..."* (Matthew 16:18), He was of course referring to the "visible church," the body. As our head has authority over our physical body, so Christ is the head of the church, having authority over it and giving it direction. Jew and Gentile alike are reconciled into that one body.

In Ephesians 5:23, we see the picture of Jesus and the church as his bride. The image and symbolism of marriage is applied to Christ and the body of believers known as the church. In the New Testament, Christ, the Bridegroom, has sacrificially and lovingly chosen the church to be His "bride" (Ephesians 5:25-27). Just as there was a betrothal period in biblical times during which the bride and groom were separated until the wedding, so is the bride of Christ separate from her Bridegroom during the church age, which we're in now.

The "bride's" responsibility during the betrothal period is to be faithful to Him, we read in II Corinthians 11:2 and Ephesians 5:24. At the Second Coming of Christ, the church ("bride") will be united with the Bridegroom, the official "wedding ceremony" will take place, and with it, the eternal union of Christ and His bride will be actualized (Revelation 19:7-9; 21:1-2).

At that time, all believers will inhabit the heavenly city known as the New Jerusalem. In the Revelation, St. John sees the city coming down from Heaven adorned "as a bride," meaning that the redeemed of the Lord, will be holy and pure, wearing white garments of holiness and righteousness.

Some have misinterpreted Revelation 19:9 to mean the holy city is the bride of Christ, but that can't be true because Christ died for His *people*, not for a *city*. The city is called the bride because it encompasses all who *are* the bride, just as all the students of a school are sometimes called "the school."

Today, the church waits for Jesus to return and take the bride to be with him, after which the glory of the millennial kingdom will follow. What a beautiful picture!

Jesus is the cornerstone of the church (Ephesians 2:20). A cornerstone is the primary stone at a place in a building where the architect fixes a standard for the load of the walls and cross-walls throughout. Likewise, the whole building of the church is fitted together (Ephesians 2:21) and constructed by no one except Jesus Himself.[3] Just like we Texans watched the construction of the new Dallas Cowboys stadium, so the church is coming together as a living organism, growing as new believers are added to the "building." It's exciting to see the "building" going up!

Peter described the foundation of the church as a building and a priesthood, stating, *"You also, as living stones, are being built up as a spiritual house for a holy priesthood* (I Peter 29)." How exciting is that?

John tops off that analogy in telling us that we are both a king and a priest (Revelation 1:6). We have all that and an everpresent access to the King of Kings, the Chief Priest, Jesus Christ as well. We are truly blessed!

> *"Gentiles and Jews will become one flock with one Shepherd."*
> *Jesus, in John 10:16*

The New Testament calls a congregation a "flock" in John 10:16, and the Old Testament tells us that Jesus is our Shepherd in the 23rd Psalm. Jesus calls all to His flock, Jews and Gentiles alike, *"I have other sheep* [Gentiles] *which are not of this fold* [Israel]; *I must bring them also and they will hear my voice: and they will become one flock* [the church] *with one Shepherd"* (John 10:16).

The intimacy with Jesus which compels the sheep to respond to Jesus' voice is best reflected in the passage of John 10:7, where Jesus tells us that He is *"the door of the sheep."* In those days, the shepherd would herd the flock to a fenced-in paddock for the night, and while they rested, he would lay across the threshold or "doorway" as in the open part of a rock fence, protecting them. No predator could get to the sheep without first encountering Him. God has made that very same provision for the believer. So sleep well, my friends. Jesus is on watch! How good is that? Come on!

Finally, in John 15, Jesus says the church is but a branch in Him, the Vine. *"I am the vine, you are the branches. He that abideth in me, and I in him, the same bringeth forth much fruit"* (John 15:5). Jesus uses the Greek word *meno,* to "abide," meaning to *remain,* virtually to *live in me.*[4] It's a continuous eternal walk that started the day one was born-again.[5]

Every Christian soon learns of the perfect definition of the church in Matthew 18:20, when Jesus said, *"Wherever two or more are gathered together in my name, there I am in the midst of them,"* to which Albert Barnes adds, *"by my authority, acting for me in my church."*[6]

Of course, this quote is the quintessential comment of every pastor who arrives at a poorly attended worship service. Even so, it's a very good definition of the body of Christ. The life of the Church is the very life of Christ Himself.[7]

Bride, priesthood, flock, branch or body, Jesus is ours, and we are His!

Distinctives of the Church

The early church was doctrinally pure. One of the first characteristics of the church in Jerusalem was that they *"continued steadfastly in the apostles' doctrine"* (Acts 2:42). The apostles taught doctrinal content to the early Christians but they also applied it to life. Being under the discipline of the Word of God helps the church grow and provides for good doctrine in its foundation, definition and ability to rightly divide the truth.

> *The Word of God provides the best foundation for growth and doctrine, rightly dividing the Truth.*

In his letter to Timothy, Paul writes, *"Study to shew thyself approved unto God, a workman that needeth not to be ashamed, rightly dividing the word of truth"* (II Timothy 2:15). The Greek word translated "rightly dividing" is *orthotomeo*, and is used only this one time in the Scriptures. It means *"to make straight,"* much like an orthodontist rightly divides and makes straight the teeth of children. Remember your braces? Bet you never thought of them as doctrinal!

Functions of the Church

Today's church could find their "mission statement" in Acts 2:42: *"They devoted themselves to the apostles' teaching and to the fellowship, to the breaking of bread and to prayer."* According to this verse, the functions of the church should be:

teaching biblical doctrine,

providing a place of fellowship for believers,

observing the Lord's supper, and

praying, which must include ministry.

Church teaching in the Bible is the antidote to false doctrine (I Timothy 1:3). And that's a fact.

Teaching produces love amongst church members and believers.

It provides spiritual nourishment for a spiritually starved world.

It produces godliness as nothing else can.

It provides a submission and a proper focus on life. That Bible focus is what I recently told a group of high school graduating seniors to seek, and it's all substantiated by I Timothy 1:1-6, 4:6-16 and 5:17-6:2.

Church teaching in the Bible grounds us in our faith. Ephesians 4:14 tells us, *"Then we will no longer be infants, tossed back and forth by the waves, and blown here and there by every wind of teaching and by the cunning and craftiness of men in their deceitful scheming."*

Church fellowship is the place where Christians can

devote themselves to the well-being of one another,

honor one another (Romans 12:10),

instruct one another (Romans 15:14),

be are kind and compassionate to one another (Ephesians 4:32),

encourage one another (I Thessalonians 5:11) and most importantly, as Jesus instructed us, the church is where we learn how to love one another (I John 3:11). No amount of secular teaching can accomplish that.

I don't know if I'd even be here to day, if it wasn't for my sister Susie and Rev. Anderson of the non-denominational Bible Fellowship in East Paterson, New Jersey. The town was in a downward spiral, a working class neighborhood rife with sinful temptations for a 13-year-old boy. Susie encouraged me to go to church there, and on Saturdays, Rev. Anderson would take a few kids in his car to some retreat or such. Those were fun trips.

I remember one time feeling so naughty because I was kissing a girl in the back seat as he was driving. It was innocent, and he knew it, and I knew he knew it. But we had fun and for a few hours, Anderson kept a half-dozen kids from the evils of that scary suburb, taking us instead to a place where we could fellowship with other good kids and come to know God. That's Matthew 28:19-20 in action, folks. That's what church is meant to be!

Church is where we share each other. We all learned soon after our conversion of the Greek word, *koinonia,* which means literally to share ourselves. It means to share love, of course, but also to share what we have, as in material things, to help spread the Good News of Jesus. For Pastor Anderson, it was a few gallons of gas and a few hours of his time.

Church is a place to build up one another, refrain from judging one another, and keep with one another the unity of the faith for which Christ prayed in Gethsemane (John 17), for which Paul pleads (Philippians 2:1-4). Heaven's like that!

The church is where we learn how to love one another.
(I John 3:11)

Church is a place where believers break bread together, including the celebration of Christ's death and shed blood on our behalf (I Corinthians 11:23-26). By enjoying meals together, we the church promote Christian fellowship.

I learned as a young Naval Aviation Cadet, at age 20, that First Baptist Church in Milton, Florida, served southern-style home cooking on Wednesday nights. OK, they also had some cute teen-age girls. But, I've got to tell you, that's why I'm saved today. I came for the chicken, but God had other food in store for me - the food of His Word. I'm so glad to be saved, but I can still taste that chicken! Hey, I'm just bein' honest!

Church is a place of prayer, according to Acts 2:42. Corporate prayer. Individual prayer. The church is a place that promotes prayer, teaches prayer and practices prayer. Paul in Philippians 4:6-7 encourages us, *"Do not be anxious about anything, but in everything, by prayer and petition, with thanksgiving, present your requests to God. And the peace of God, which transcends all understanding, will guard your hearts and your minds in Christ Jesus."* That's just great counsel, and we all heard it first in church.

Of course, the duty of every Christian church member is to accomplish the Great Commission of proclaiming the gospel of salvation through Jesus Christ (Matthew 28:18-20 and Acts 1:8). The church is a place of faith in sharing the gospel through word and deed. The church is a lighthouse in the community, pointing people toward our Lord and Savior Jesus Christ, the true Lighthouse for every sinner.

When our gospel ministry *"Buddy Merrick & Praise"* was on the road, touring and singing the gospel to thousands across the country, we particularly loved singing one of the first songs we ever presented in concert, *The Lighthouse,* originally recorded by *The Florida Boys.* How true its words rang in our heart:

"There's a Lighthouse on the hillside
That overlooks life's sea.
When I'm tossed about, it sends out a light,
So that I might see.
And the light that shines in darkness now
Will safely lead me o'er.

Walk in Fellowship

> *If it wasn't for the Lighthouse,*
> *My ship would be no more.*
> *And I thank God for the Lighthouse,*
> *I owe my life to Him.*
> *Jesus is the Lighthouse*
> *And from the rocks of sin*
> *He has shone a bright light all around me*
> *That I could clearly see,*
> *If it wasn't for the Lighthouse*
> *Tell me where would this ship be."*[8]

As we led into the refrain at the end of each verse with the lyrics, *"If it wasn't for the Lighthouse...,"* David would interject, *"Tell me..."* followed by the full trio joining in the full crescendo complement, *"...Where would this ship be?"* Yes, we wonder how much ministry was done as we encouraged our audiences to *"tell..."* others about the Lighthouse, Jesus Christ. How fun it was to sing God's praises with His church!

The church is established for the function of ministry. James, the brother of Jesus, counsels us in James 1:27, he says, *"[Here's the definition of] pure religion... to look after orphans and widows in their distress and to keep oneself from being polluted by the world."*

Thus, the church exists to fellowship and minister to those in need, not only by sharing the gospel, but also by providing for physical needs, food, clothing and shelter as necessary and appropriate.

The church must also equip believers in Christ with the tools they need to overcome sin and remain free from the pollution of the world. This is done by biblical teaching and Christian fellowship.

> *The church is the body of Christ doing the things that Jesus Christ would do if He were here physically on the earth. That's the purpose of the church.*

The church is God's hands, mouth and feet in this world, the body of Christ (I Corinthians 12:12-27), doing the things that Jesus Christ would do if He were here physically on the earth. That's the purpose of the church.

Look at all we gain from being in fellowship with the church! How sad it is that some deprive themselves of all this, just to get a few more minutes of sleep on a Sunday morning!

Leaders of the Church

God was very clear in His Word about how His church on Earth is to be organized and managed.

First, Christ is the head of the church and its supreme authority (Ephesians 1:22; 4:15 and Colossians 1:18).

Second, the local church is autonomous, free from any external authority or control, self-governing, and free from the interference of any hierarchy of individuals or organizations (Titus 1:5). Should I add, "or politics?" OK, another book, another time.

Third, the church is governed by spiritual leadership consisting of two main offices, elders and deacons.

"Elders" were the leaders among the Israelites since the time of Moses. They made political decisions (II Samuel 5:3, 17:4, 17:15), advised the king in later history (I Kings 20:7), and represented the people concerning spiritual matters (Exodus 7:17:5-6, 24:1, 9, and Numbers 11:16, 24-25). The early Greek translation of the Old Testament, the *Septuagint,* used the Greek word *presbuteros* meaning "elder," and this same Greek word is used in the New Testament as well.

The New Testament refers a number of times to elders who served in the role of church leadership (Acts 14:23, 15:2, 20:17; Titus 1:5; James 5:14). Each church had more than one, as the word is usually found in the plural. The only exceptions refer to cases in which one elder is being singled out for some reason (I Timothy 5:1, 19). In the Jerusalem church, elders were part of the leadership along with the apostles as well (Acts 15:2-16:4).

The position of elders or presbyters was equal to the position of the "overseer," in Greek the *episkopos,* whom we might call a "bishop" (I Timothy 5:17). In Philippians 1:1, Paul greets the bishops and deacons but doesn't mention the elders, presumably because the elders are the same as the bishops. Likewise, I Timothy 3:2 and 8 gives the qualifications of bishops and deacons but not of elders. Titus 1:5-7 seems also to tie these two terms together.

Elders have the authority and duty to distribute money (Acts 11:30), make decisions about doctrine (Acts 15:2) and to visit the sick and pray for them, offering counsel and encouragement (James 5:14).[9] They are respected (I Timothy 5:17), but not dictatorial (I Peter 5:1-3).

The qualifications of elders are set forth in I Timothy 3:1-7 and Titus 1:5-9. The elder must be

> above reproach,
> of one wife,
> temperate,
> sober,
> prudent,
> discreet,
> hospitable,
> a teacher with sound doctrine,
> respected,
> well-balanced,
> not addicted to wine,
> gentle,
> uncontentious,
> not greedy,
> a good manager of his own household and
> not a new convert.

The elder shepherds the flock, teaches, leads and guards the doctrine.

The position of "deacon," from the Greek word *diakonos,* meaning "through the dirt," was one of servant leadership to the church. Does that mean they should do the dirty work? Well, you can kid them the next time you see them.

Deacons are servants.
I Timothy 3: 8-13

Deacons are separate from elders. While qualified in many ways similar to elders (I Timothy 3:8-13), deacons are servants. They assist the church in whatever is needed, as recorded in Acts chapter 6.

12 Ways to Walk with God

The qualifications of the office of deacon are defined in I Timothy 3:8-13. Deacons are

>men of dignity,
>serious,
>worthy,
>respected,
>not addicted to wine,
>not dishonest,
>not greedy.

Deacons hold to the mystery of faith and practice what they proclaim. They are

>tested and approved,
>not divorced,
>with one wife and
>good managers of their household.

The "pastor" is the leader of the church. Curiously, the word pastor is found only once in the New Testament, in Ephesians 4:11: *"It was he who gave some to be apostles, some to be prophets, some to be evangelists, and some to be pastors and teachers."* Most associate the two terms "pastors" and "teachers" as referring to a single position, a pastor-teacher. That's a good thing. It's likely that a pastor-teacher was the spiritual shepherd of a particular local church back in the day.

Whether elders, deacons or pastor, the Bible tells all of us to serve. Even you and me.

These qualifications also presuppose, of course, that one seeking such an office is a born-again believer and Walks With God, in submission to God's Word. Being faithful to the Word enables these men to be able to exhort and to teach and to convince others of God's truth, as God continually enlightens them through their own walk and study.

These aren't offices to be taken lightly. Jesus' brother James said, *"Not many of you should presume to be teachers, my brothers, because you know that we who teach will be judged more strictly"* (James 3:1 NIV).

Peter calls the Lord Jesus the *"Shepherd and Bishop of our souls"* (I Peter 2:25). The two words used here are interesting. The word "Shepherd" is the Greek word *"poimen,"* and it is also translated "pastor"

(Ephesians 4:11). This *poimen* is one who tends herds or flocks and is used metaphorically of Christian pastors because pastors *("bishops")* should guide as well as feed the flock the bread of life, the Word of God.

Clearly, these are important offices in the church.

Organization of the Church

God gifted particular elders with the "teaching gifts" while He gifted others with other "spiritual gifts" (Romans 12:3-8; Ephesians 4:11), calling them into a ministry in which they will use those gifts (Acts 13:1).

So, while one elder may do the majority of visiting members because he has the gift of compassion, another may minister in the sense of handling the organizational details. Many churches that are organized with a pastor and deacon board perform the functions of a plurality of elders in that they share the ministry load and work together in some decision making. In Scripture, there was also much congregational input into decisions.

Therefore, it's just unscriptural for a church to have a dictator-type leader who makes all the decisions by himself, or for a congregation-ruled church that doesn't respect or give weight to the elders' or church leaders' input. We need to avoid that.

Government in the Church

The word "episcopal" comes from the Greek word, *episkopos,* meaning "overseer," translated "bishop" in the King James Version of the Bible. The simplest form of an episcopal church is the Methodist church and some Lutheran bodies. More complex is the Episcopal, Anglican church. The most complex is the Roman Catholic church, with the ultimate authority vested in the Bishop of Rome, today Pope Frances I[10].

In the episcopal church, the bishops oversee a group of churches. Bishops ordain priests and ministers. Roman Catholics claim authority derived from apostolic succession from Peter himself, who is declared to be the first Pope and who is buried in the foundation of St. Peter's Basilica in Rome, the Mother Church of the Catholic faith. This form of church government arose in the second century, but adherents claim Biblical support from the fact that James was the head of the church in Jerusalem and that Timothy and Titus enjoyed positions of church authority as well.

The Presbyterian and Reformed churches are governed by elders, who emphasize a representative rule appointed by the people. The "session," which is comprised of ruling elders governs the church. Above the session is the "presbytery," including all ordained ministers or teaching elders as well as one ruling elder from each local congregation in a district. Above the presbytery is the "synod" and over the synod is the "general assembly," the highest court. The pastor serves as one of the elders.[11]

> *If you can attend a church meeting without fear of harassment, arrest, torture or death, you're more blessed than three billion people in the world.*

In Congregational church government, the authority rests with the entire congregation. Baptists, Evangelical Free, Congregational, some Lutherans and some independent churches follow this form of church government. That's why we have all those pesky business meetings!

We surely can't overlook the wonderful blessing we have in being able to worship as we choose in this great country called America! Praise the Lord for our freedom!

Ordinances of the Church

Christ instituted the Lord's Supper on the evening before his crucifixion, commanding his followers to continue to remember his sacrifice, and to observe this sacrament until his return (Matthew 26:

26-29, Mark 14:22-25 and Luke 22:14-23). Paul also rehearsed the ordinance for the church at Corinth (I Corinthians 11:23-32).

The Roman Catholic view of the Lord's Supper is called "transubstantiation," meaning a change of substance. They teach that a miracle takes place at the Eucharist, or Mass, in which the elements of the bread and wine are actually changed into the literal body and blood of the Savior.

The Lutheran view is referred to as "consubstantiation," meaning that Jesus' body and blood are actually present in the elements, but the bread and wine remain such. They don't change into literal body and blood. Martin Luther illustrated the point by stating that as heat penetrated an iron bar when placed in the fire, the bar remains iron nonetheless[13].

The Reformed Church view is also called the Calvinist view because adherents who follow John Calvin's teaching on the subject. They reject the notion of the literal presence of Christ in any sense and see the Lord's Supper as a memorial. Calvin taught that Christ *"is present and enjoyed in His entire person, both body and blood. He emphasizes the mystical communion of believers with the entire person of the Redeemer. The body and blood of Christ, though absent and locally present only in heaven, communicate a life-giving influence to the believer."*[12]

The memorial view is also called the Zwinglian view because the Swiss reformer Ulrich Zwingli is considered its exponent. Zwingli taught that there was no real presence of Christ but only a spiritual fellowship with Christ by those who partake in faith.

Scriptures teach us that the Lord's Supper is
> a remembrance of Christ's death (I Corinthians 11:24-25),
> His sacrifice (I Peter 2:24),
> His shed blood (Ephesians 1:7,
> a proclaiming of Jesus while we wait for His second coming (I Corinthians 11:26)
> and His return (Matthew 26:29).

Baptism

Christian baptism is, according to the Bible, an outward testimony of what has occurred inwardly in a believer's life. The believer is buried (in water), symbolically with Jesus, and raised up again to walk in a newness of life. It's a beautiful illustration of a believer's identification with Christ's death, burial, and resurrection. Just as Christ was dead, buried and resurrected, the believer is buried in the water and resurrected to walk in a new life. What an honor!

> *We are buried with Him in baptism and raised to walk in a brand new life!*

The Bible declares, *"Don't you know that all of us who were baptized into Christ Jesus were baptized into his death? We were therefore buried with Him through baptism into death in order that, just as Christ was raised from the dead through the glory of the Father, we too may live a new life"* (Romans 6:3-4).

In Christian baptism, there are two requirements before a person is baptized:

1) the person being baptized must have trusted in Jesus Christ as Savior, and

2) the person must understand what baptism signifies. If a person knows the Lord Jesus as Savior, understands that Christian baptism is a step of obedience in publicly proclaiming his faith in Christ and desires to be baptized, then there is no reason to prevent the believer from being baptized.

Philip, the Apostle, once traveled with an Ethiopian eunuch.[14] The Bible says Philip *"preached unto him Jesus"* (Acts 8:36-37).

When they came upon water, the man said to Philip, *"Look, here is water. Why shouldn't I be baptized?"*

And Philip said, *"If you believe with all your heart, you may."*

And he answered and said, *"I believe that Jesus Christ is the Son of God."*

One would ask any believer who hasn't been baptized, *"We've got the pool. The water is warm. What is hindering you from being baptized? Here's your chance to declare, 'I believe that Jesus Christ is the Son of God.'"* Yes! Let's do it!

According to the Bible, then, Christian baptism is important because it's

> an identification with Jesus as Lord,
>
> a step of obedience,
>
> a public declaration of faith in Christ and commitment to Him
>
> and an identification with Christ's death, burial, and resurrection.

Dunk or Sprinkle?

Churches that sprinkle with water rather than immerse the believer, are symbolizing the same thing. Still, baptism, by the very definition of the word *"baptisma"* in the Greek, is an act of immersion in water. The word "baptize" means "to submerge in water." Therefore, the symbolism of baptism by sprinkling or by pouring is difficult to envision as submerging someone in water by sprinkling water on them.

The old country preacher was baptizing one of his flock in the lake behind the church.

"Do you believe?" He asked the man.

"Yeah, I believe!" came the reply. With that he dropped him into the water, and brought him back up again.

"Do you believe?" He asked again.

"I believe!" came the reply again. With that he dropped him into the water again, and brought him back up a second time. And then, a third time!

A little louder, the preacher asked, excitedly, *"Do you be-lee-ve?*

"Yeah, I believe!" came the reply, a little louder, too.

"What do you believe?" asked the preacher.

"I believe y'all are tryin' to drown me!" said the believer.

Glug, glug. He may have missed the point of baptism.

If baptism illustrates a believer's identification with Christ's death, burial, and resurrection, then being immersed in the water pictures dying and being buried with Christ. Coming out of the water illustrates Christ's resurrection. As a result, many believe that baptism by immersion is the only method of baptism which clearly illustrates being buried with Christ and being raised with Him. But once is enough!

Baptism by immersion isn't (as some believe) a prerequisite for salvation. It's a picture of our leaving our old life and becoming a new creation (II Corinthians 5:17). Baptism illustrates this radical change that has already taken place. Still,

The Roman Catholics believe baptism is a *means* of saving grace, called *baptismal regeneration*. By God imparting His grace, sins are forgiven in the act itself. Faith isn't necessary, the act itself is sufficient.[13] Lutherans believe that faith is a prerequisite, but they don't practice immersion.

Reformed and Presbyterian churches practice baptism as a means of initiation into the covenant and a sign of salvation.[15]

Baptists and others, including me, believe that baptism is only a symbol of our salvation that has already taken place, an outward sign of an inward change. Therefore, a baptism follows a profession of faith and an acceptance of Jesus as Savior. By definition, only believers can be baptized.

Summary

The local church taught me how to fellowship with the Body of Christ. Over many years, I've learned that Jesus built this church. He's the Cornerstone. He's the Head. He's my "Door" who lays His body down that I might be secure in His love, protected from all enemies. We can find Jesus anywhere if two or more of us gather in His name.

I also know, through the Scriptures that were taught to me since I was a little boy in Fair Lawn, New Jersey, at Warren Point Presbyterian Church, that the church is a place of worship, fellowship, teaching and ministry. I'm blessed with a myriad of opportunities to tell the Good

News or to share Jesus love with others. I learned to pray in church and I learned how to sing God's praises.

I learned to minister in many ways. Some of that teaching came directly from the Holy Spirit, but some came from God's ministers, like Rev. Anderson. What an example of goodness!

I've never been a deacon or an elder, but I've been a pastor. The responsibility is awesome, but it's a calling of God, supported by His Word. It's all about loving His children.

Love is meeting needs. And, that's what a church, a pastor and a Christian are called to do.

John 15:1 says, *"Every branch in me that beareth not fruit, He [God] taketh away..."*

I recently learned that the phrase *"taketh away"* in the Greek is *airei* and may be translated "lifts up," versus "discarded" as I'd always believed. I actually raised grapes at one time in my life, so I know how the branches tend to droop, especially when laden down with fruit. When a branch sags, the accomplished vinekeeper places a stick or stone underneath the branch to "lift it up," and by doing that, it'll produce more fruit. Hey, I did that myself! God is my Able Vinekeeper, who provides a "holy stick" to lift me up and in doing that, He enjoys watching me bear more fruit than I would if I was laden down and simply left to droop. Of course, the Vinekeeper also prunes the dead or unproducing parts away from the good branches, so that they might, again, produce more and better fruit. How wonderful is that!

Jesus built this church on love.

I'm "propped up" by Jesus! That should be a gospel song, shouldn't it? *"Propped Up By Jesus!"* Wow, I can almost hear the tune!

My wife, Carol, and I used to sing a duet of a song written by a dear friend, Joel Hemphill, about the church's true mission, love: Joel asked and taught:

> *"Do you ever just get to wond'rin'*
> *'bout the way things are today?*
> *So many on board the gospel ship trying to row it a different way.*
> *If we'd all pull together like a family me and you*

> *We'd come a lot closer to doin' what the Lord called us to do.*
> *Jesus built this church on love, on love.*
> *That's what it's all about.*
> *Tryin' to get everybody saved, not to keep anybody out.*
> *The door's wide open and just as big*
> *as the Father's heart above.*
> *I'm glad He said, 'Whosoever will,'*
> *Jesus built this church on love."*[16]

A Church-goer wrote a letter to the editor of a newspaper and complained that it made no sense to go to church every Sunday.

"I've gone for 30 years now," he wrote, *"and in that time I have heard something like 3,000 sermons. But for the life of me, I can't remember a single one of them. So, I think I'm wasting my time and the pastors are wasting theirs by giving sermons at all."*

This started a real controversy in the "Letters to the Editor" column, much to the delight of the newspaper. It went on for weeks until someone wrote this great response:

"I've been married for 30 years now. In that time my wife has cooked some 32,000 meals. But for the life of me, I cannot recall the entire menu for a single one of those meals. However, I do know this: They all nourished me and gave me the strength I needed to do my work. If my wife had not given me those meals, I would be physically dead today.

"Likewise, if I had not gone to church for nourishment, I would be spiritually dead today! God lives in my church and I'm so glad He does."

That's what fellowship in the church, the Lighthouse, does for us all!

---

[1] Thiessen, Henry C., *Christian Theology*, 3 viols. (Grand Rapids: Baker, 1985), 3:1043-48; cf. Douglas Kelley et al, eds., *The Westminister Confession of Faith*, 2nd ed. (Greenwood, SC: Attic, 1981), pg. 44.

[2] Saucy, Robert L., *The Church in God's Program* (Chicago: Moody, 1972), pg. 11.

[3] Robertson, A. T., *Word Pictures in the New Testament*, 6 viols. (Nashville: Broadman, 1931), 4:528-529.

[4] Arndt, William F. and Gingrich, Wilbur F., *A Greek-English Lexicon of the New Testament and Other Early Christian Literature*, rev. F. Wilbur Gingrich and Frederick W. Danker (Chicago: University of Chicago, 1979), pg. 505.

[5] Spiker, Louis C., *No Instant Grapes in God's Vineyard* (Valley Forge, PA: Judson Press, 1982), pg. 13. This wonderful little book was among those I purchased during my studies for a Master of Divinity degree at Southern Seminary in Louisville, KY. I have loved John 15 ever since.

[6] Barnes, Albert, *Barnes Notes On The Bible*, 1834.

[7] Towns, Elmer L., *Concise Bible Doctrines* (Chattanooga, TN: AMG Publishers, 2006), pg. 326.

[8] Written by one of the greatest gospel song writers ever, Ronnie Hinson © 1971. I recorded the song for a compilation cassette for Waikiki Baptist Church in 1987 under the direction of Wayne Meeds.

[9] Blue, J. Ronald, "James," *The Bible Knowledge Commentary*, 2:834-835.

[10] Erickson, Millard J., *Christian Theology*, 3 vols. (Grand Rapids: Baker, 1985), 3:1070.

[11] Saucy, *The Church in God's Program*, pg. 112.

[12] Erickson, *Christian Theology*, 3:1117.

[13] Berkof, Louis, *Systematic Theology* (Grand Rapids: Eerdmans, 1941), pg. 653.

[14] A eunuch was a man who had been castrated, a common thing for the day, especially (or formerly) for some office such as a guard in a harem. This eunuch, from Ethiopia was a black man, conversing with Philip, who was from Mid-Eastern Bethsaida, the same hometown as Andrew and Peter.

[15] Erickson, *Christian Theology*, 3:1090.

[16] Hemphill, Joel, *"Jesus Build This Church On Love,"* (Nashville, TN: Brentwood-Benson Music Publishing, 1986).

XI. Walk in God's Image

Creationism - In the Beginning, God

Preface

God was talking to one of the angels, and said, "I've just created this spinning earth, which creates light within a 24-hour period, alternating light and darkness!"
The angel said, "What are you going to do now?"
God said, "I think I'm going to call it a day."

So, how did it all start?

"Creationism" is the doctrine of origins, the belief that humanity, life, our world and our universe were created in their original form by God. God alone, with no other. Creation was achieved out of nothing but the spoken word of God. He tells us that in Genesis chapters one and two.

In man's human reasoning, creationism covers an extraordinary wide range of beliefs and interpretations.

Christian creationism is based on a literal reading of the Genesis account.

Outside of Christianity, the term creationism is commonly used by folks who, for a religiously motivated reasons, reject evolution as an explanation of origins. Include me in that and I'll tell you why.

First, let's see what Christians believe: The doctrine of creationism teaches that all things were created substantially as they now exist by God the omnipotent Creator.

They are not gradually evolved or developed as evolutionists believe.

Creationism is the true story of the creation of the universe as it is recounted in the Bible, especially in that first chapter. Genesis 1:1 says, *"In the beginning God created the heavens and the earth."* Did you know that virtually every major version of the Bible translates that verse exactly the same, word for word? That's pretty definitive!

Every day, God immediately creates, out of nothing, a new human soul for each individual born. It happened at the beginning, it's happening today, and it'll happen tomorrow. God is still making babies, and *souls*.

Then, there's the other side: "Evolution" is the theory of beginnings that opposes Christian creationism, a hypothesis first proposed in the nineteenth century by Charles Darwin. He postulated that the earth's species have changed and diversified through time under the influence of natural selection. Darwin proposed that life on Earth "evolved" in three stages:

First came chemical evolution in which organic molecules were formed, the so-called primordial ooze theory, or *abiogenesis,* a postulation of how life on Earth could have arisen from inanimate matter. Where did the inanimate matter come from? There are no answers to this question (except that God created). Don't confuse this "start-up" with evolution, which is the study of how groups of living things, somehow here, change over time.

Second was the development of single cells capable of reproducing themselves.

Finally, single cells led to the development of complex organisms capable of sexual reproduction.

Evolution is generally accepted as "fact" by scientists today, although debates continue over what precise mechanisms are involved in the process.

Remember learning about this in school?

The truth is, if one believes the Bible,
> Creationism is right.
> Evolution is wrong.

Walk in God's Image

Still, over the centuries, thinkers have "created" theories to modify the truth, or as they would say, interpret it, so that two very opposing theories could somehow homogenize.

Through the 19th century, the term creationism referred to direct creation of individual souls by God. It contrasted with "traducianism," the doctrine that human souls are produced by the act of generation by parents and nothing else.

By 1929, several U.S. states passed laws against the teaching of evolution in public schools, as upheld in the *Scopes Monkey Trial*, which made it unlawful in Tennessee *"to teach any theory that denies the story of the Divine Creation of man as taught in the Bible, and to teach instead that man has descended from a lower order of animals."*[1]

Evolution was omitted entirely from many school textbooks, but in the last 40 years we've seen renewed efforts to redefine creationism as flood geology, creation science and so-called intelligent design.

"Life" is the time God gives you to determine how you spend eternity.

Such beliefs include "Young Earth Creationism," proponents of which believe that the earth is thousands rather than billions of years old. These folks typically believe that the days in Genesis Chapter One are literally twenty-four hours in length.

"Old Earth Creationists" accept geological findings and other methods of dating the earth, and believe that while these findings do not contradict the Genesis account, they do reject evolution. We'll talk more about that later in this book.

The theory of "Theistic Evolution" attempts to be more compatible with the scientific view of evolution and the age of the earth.

And then, there are other religious people who support creation, but only in allegorical interpretations of the Word. The most notable disputes concern the effects of evolution on the development of living organisms, the idea of common descent, the geologic history of the earth, the formation of the solar system and the origin of the universe.

Creationism as a doctrine must consider natural theology, evolution, creation science and intelligent design, along with theistic evolution, young earth creationism, modern geocentrism, omphalos hypothesis, old earth creationism, gap creationism, day-age creationism, progressive creationism and neo-creationism and creationism. *Whew!*

Early Beliefs

The early Christian church fathers were more concerned with the spiritual meaning of creationism than the literal, without denying the literal meaning. In fact, Jews and Christians both considered the idea of creation as an allegory (versus history) long before the development of Darwin's theory of evolution, including the thinking of theologians like Philo of Alexandria and St. Augustine.

In about 50 AD, Philo described creation as happening simultaneously, with the six days of creation simply meeting a need for order.

In about 60 AD, the apostle Paul described Genesis 2:24, which says *"two shall become one flesh,"* as a descriptive allegory meaning Christ and the Church. He repeated that position in Ephesians 5 and to the church at Corinth, saying, *"He who is united with the Lord becomes one spirit with Him"* (I Corinthians 6:17).

In about 250 AD, the theologian Origen, one of the most distinguished of the early fathers of the Christian Church, declared that the physical world is literally a creation of God, but did not take the chronology or the days as literal.

In about 430 AD, philosopher and theologian St. Augustine of Hippo, profoundly influenced the medieval world view. He insisted in his writing, *"The Literal Meaning of Genesis,"* that Genesis describes the creation of physical things, with the days being "categories" of a logical framework which has nothing to do with time.[2]

Time was moving on, folks.

But, God had not changed.

In about 1517, Martin Luther and the Protestant Reformation brought a new emphasis on creationism, when Luther advocated that creation took six literal days about 6000 years ago, and claimed that

"Moses wrote that uneducated men might have clear accounts of creation." In other words, believe Moses.

In about 1564, theologian and pastor John Calvin also rejected instantaneous creation, but criticized those who, contradicting the contemporary understanding of nature, asserted that there are *"waters above the heavens."*[3]

In 1605, Francis Bacon emphasized that God, working in nature, teaches us how to interpret the Word of God in the Bible, and his Baconian method introduced the empirical approach which became central to modern science.

Natural Theology

So, men studied nature with the expectation of finding evidence supporting Christianity, making numerous attempts made to reconcile new knowledge with Noah's Flood. "Catastrophism" was favored in England as supporting the Biblical flood, but this was found to be untenable and by 1850 all geologists and most evangelical Christians had adopted various forms of Old Earth Creationism, while still continuing to firmly reject evolution.

> *It wasn't raining when Noah built the ark.*

As for Noah's Flood? Well, here's a few things we could've learned from Noah:

> Plan ahead. It wasn't raining when Noah built the Ark.
>
> Don't feel lonely: We're all in the same boat.
>
> Stay fit. When you're 60 years old, someone may ask you to do something really big.
>
> Don't listen to critics; just get on with the job that needs to be done.
>
> Don't miss the boat.
>
> Build your future on high ground.
>
> For safety's sake, travel in pairs.

Speed isn't always an advantage. The snails were on board with the cheetahs.

When you're stressed, float awhile.

Most important: Remember, the Ark was built by amateurs, the Titanic was built by professionals.

Evolution: True science fiction.

Human Evolution

Then came Darwin in 1859. His work, *"On the Origin of Species,"* advanced his so-called "evidence" of evolution and gradually convinced scientists that evolution occurs. After World War I, a popular belief that German aggression resulted from Darwin's theory of *"survival of the fittest"* inspired U. S. Presidential nominee and devout Presbyterian, William Jennings Bryan, to actually campaign against the teaching of Darwin's ideas about human evolution. Bryan might have been right, but he still lost the election to William McKinley.

Intelligent Design

Because "creation science" could no longer be taught in public schools, the creation science school textbook, *"Of Pandas and People: The Central Question of Biological Origins,"* changed all references to creationism to "intelligent design."[4] Published by the Texas-based Foundation for Thought and Ethics in 1989, it espoused the idea of intelligent design, namely, that life shows evidence of being designed by an intelligent agent, God. It disputes Darwin's unguided "macroevolution [the opposite of intelligent design]," and explains origins from the biological point of view:

"missing links" in the fossil records,

molecular comparisons in genetics,
genes-alone-don't-control development,
analogy and homology,
alleged vestigial organs and the like.

It asks the obvious question of, "Where did the unbelievable intricacy of molecular machinery necessary for life come from in the first place?"

We know the answer to that, right?

God.

Intelligent design is still considered to be pseudoscience (a method having no scientific basis by the scientific community), primarily because it invokes supernatural powers, makes no predictions, and can't be verified through repeatable experiments. In 2007, a third edition of the book was published under the title, *"The Design of Life: Discovering Signs of Intelligence in Biological Systems."*[5]

Often called "ID," intelligent design claims that certain features of the universe and of living things are best explained by an intelligent cause, not an undirected process such as natural selection. It's widely accepted in the scientific and academic communities that intelligent design is a form of creationism, and some have even gone as far as referring to it as "intelligent design creationism."[6]

ID originated as a re-branding of creation science in an attempt to get around a series of court decisions that ruled out the teaching of creationism in U.S. public schools. In the United States, teaching of intelligent design in public schools has been decisively ruled to be in violation of the Establishment Clause of the First Amendment to the United States Constitution, by a Federal District court. In a trial titled, *Kitzmiller v. Dover Area School District*, the court found that intelligent design is not science and *"cannot uncouple itself from its creationist, and thus religious, antecedents,"* and hence can't be taught as an alternative to evolution in public school science classrooms under the jurisdiction of that court.[7]

Theistic Evolution

"Theistic evolution" hypothesizes that classical religious teachings about God and creation are compatible with modern scientific theory, even (specifically) evolution. It's also known as "evolutionary creation." In *Evolution Vs. Creationism,* Eugene Scott and Niles Eldredge state that it is in fact a type of evolution.[8]

Theistic evolution generally views evolution as a tool used by God. Theistic evolution believes that the complexity of the entire physical universe, created by God, evolved from "fundamental particles" in processes. Life forms developed in biological evolution and, in the same way, the origin of life by natural causes resulted from these laws.

Protestant seminaries, at least the majority of mainline ones, teach theistic evolution today, probably because it's God-based.

God is still the Creator.

Catholics, on the other hand, believe that human evolution is not a matter of religious teaching, so therefore to them it must stand or fall on its own scientific merits. Roman Catholic schools teach evolution on the belief that scientific knowledge does not extend beyond the physical. Scientific truth and religious truth are separate and therefore can't be in conflict. Theistic evolution, they say, can be described as "creationism" in its belief that divine intervention brought about the origin of life, or that divine laws govern formation of species. Still, many creationists would deny that the Roman Catholic position is creationism at all. In the creation-evolution controversy, its proponents generally take the "evolutionist" side.

While supporting the methodologies of modern science, the proponents of theistic evolution reject the implication taken by atheists that this gives credence to "ontological materialism," a metaphysics study of existence. Modern philosophers of science, including atheists, suggest that *"observable events in nature should be explained by natural causes,"* without any assumptions of the actual existence or non-existence of the supernatural. So, in their beliefs, the miracle of life is no miracle at all!

Christian Creationism

There are a ton of theories about creationism (as it differs from evolutionism), including Young Earth and Old Earth creationism, Gap creationism, Day-age creationism, Progressive creationism, Neo-Creationism, the "Omphalos hypothesis," Modern geocentrism, Creation science, Islamic creationism, Judaic creationism and Scientific Critique theories, among others.

OK, so how do we make this simple? Well, if God is real, then He is the Author and Finisher of our faith, and the Source of everything, and that's pretty absolute. Plus, John 1:3 tells us, *"All things were made by Him, and without Him, was not anything made that was made."* How inclusive is that?

> *"All things were made by Him, and without Him, was not anything made that was made."*

Still, hang on while we peruse some of the thinkers' thinking:

Young Earth and Old Earth

"Young Earth" creationism is the belief that the earth was created by God within the last ten thousand years, literally as described in Genesis, within the approximate time frame of biblical genealogies. Young Earth creationists often believe that the universe has a similar age as the earth, as in *"the heavens and the earth."* Other Young Earth creationists believe that the earth and the universe were created with the *appearance* of age, so that the world appears to be much older than it is, and that this appearance is what gives the geological findings and other methods of dating the earth and the universe their much longer timelines. The Young Earth creationism is probably the most influential brand of creationism today.

"Old Earth" creationism holds that the physical universe was created by God, but that the creation event of Genesis is not to be taken strictly literally. This group generally believes that the age of the universe and the age of the earth are just as they are described by astronomers and geologists, but that details of modern evolutionary theory are questionable.

Old-Earth creationism itself comes in at least four types:

"Gap" creationism, also called "Restitution" creationism. This theory holds that life was recently created on a pre-existing old earth, based on a particular interpretation of Genesis 1:1-2. It demands that the words "formless" and "void" in fact denote waste and ruin, assuming as a foundation the original Hebrew words and the places in the Old Testament where these words are used. Genesis 1:1 is consequently translated: *"In the beginning God created the heavens and the earth,"* meaning an original act of creation. Genesis 1:2 adds, *"And the earth was without form, and void; and darkness was upon the face of the deep. And the Spirit of God moved upon the face of the waters."* Thus, the six days of creation start sometime *after* the earth was "without form and void." This allows an indefinite "gap" of time to be inserted after the original creation of the universe, but prior to creation week when present biological species and humanity were created. Gap theorists can therefore agree with the scientific consensus regarding the age of the earth and universe, while maintaining a literal interpretation of the Biblical text.

Some gap theorists expand this basic theory by proposing a "primordial creation" of basic biological life within the "gap" of time. This is interpreted from the account of II Peter 3:3-7, which references *"the world that then was, being overflowed with water, perished..."* Discoveries of fossils and archaeological ruins older than 10,000 years are generally ascribed to this *"world that then was"*, which may also be associated with Lucifer's rebellion. These views became popular with publications of Hebrew lexicons such as the *Strong's Concordance*, and Bible commentaries such as the *Scofield Reference Bible* and the *Companion Bible*.

Herbert W. Armstrong and Jimmy Swaggart have supported the gap theory.

The second Old Earth theory, "Day-age" creationism, states that the "six days" in the Book of Genesis are not ordinary twenty-four-hour days, but rather much longer periods. For instance, each "day" of creation could actually be the equivalent of millions, or billions of years in an "age" of human time. This theory often states that the Hebrew word *"yôm"* in the context of Genesis 1, can be properly interpreted as "age." Some adherents claim we are still living in the seventh age or seventh "day." The Day-age theory is supported by the Mormons, who teach that the earth was created in six creative "periods."

The third Old Earth theory, "Progressive" creationism, holds that species have changed or evolved in a process continuously guided by God, with various ideas as to how the process operated. Still, it's generally believed that God directly intervened in the natural order at key moments in the history of Life. This view accepts most of modern physical science including the age of the earth, but rejects much of modern evolutionary biology or looks to it for evidence that evolution by natural selection alone is incorrect.

Progressive creationism is the most common Old-Earth creationism view today. It accepts most of modern physical science, even viewing the Big Bang as evidence of the creative power of God, but rejects much of modern biology. (The Big Bang theory asserts that our entire universe was created when a tiny (billions of times smaller than a proton), super-dense, super-hot mass exploded and began expanding very rapidly, eventually cooling and forming into the stars and galaxies with which we are familiar. This event is said to have happened approximately 15 billion years ago.)

Progressive creationists generally believe that God created "kinds" of organisms sequentially, in the order seen in the fossil record, but say that the newer kinds are specially created, not genetically related to older kinds.

God is still the Creator.

Progressive creationism can be viewed together with the God's Word in Genesis, such as the day-age framework, metaphoric and poetic views. But, because this view of natural history runs counter to current scientific understanding, it's unsupported by scientific journals and therefore, it's considered pseudoscience. Organizations such as the group, Reasons to Believe, founded by Hugh Ross, promote this theory.

The fourth Old Earth theory, "Neo-Creationism," attempts to restate creationism in terms more likely to be well received by the public, education policy makers and the scientific community by re-framing the debate. Its proponents believe that orthodox science is actually an atheistic religion in itself.

They argue that the scientific method excludes certain explanations of phenomena, particularly the supernatural elements. Science, as an "atheistic enterprise," is at the root of many of contemporary society's ills including social unrest and family breakdown.

It's easy to agree with that!

The most recognized form of Neo-Creationism in the United States is the intelligent design movement, of course. Unlike their philosophical ancestors, Neo-Creationists don't believe in many of the traditional cornerstones of creationism such as Young Earth or in a dogmatically literal interpretation of the Bible.

Common to all forms of Neo-Creationism is a rejection of naturalism, usually made together with a tacit admission of supernaturalism and an opposition to Darwinism and evolution.

Here are a few more theories:

The "Omphalos hypothesis" was named after the title of an 1857 book, *"Omphalos,"* by Philip Henry Gosse, in which Gosse argued that in order for the world to be "functional", God must have created the earth with mountains and canyons, trees with growth rings, Adam and Eve with hair, fingernails, and navels (omphalos is Greek for "navel"), and that therefore no evidence that we can see of the presumed age of the earth and universe can really be taken as reliable. The idea has seen some revival in the twentieth century by some modern creationists, who've extended the argument to light that appears to originate in far-off stars and galaxies.[9]

"Modern geocentrism" holds that God recently created a spherical world, and placed it in the center of the universe. The Sun, planets and everything else in the universe revolve around the earth.

"Creation science" is the attempt to present scientific evidence, interpreted with self-evident or universally recognized truths of Genesis, that supports the claims of creationism.

"Islamic creationism" is a belief that the universe and all humanity was directly created by God as explained in the Qur'an. While contemporary Islam tends to take religious texts literally, it usually views Genesis and all of the Bible as a corrupted version of God's message, one of the problems of the whole religion of Islam. The creation accounts in the Qur'an are more vague and allow for a wider range of interpretations than those in Genesis and other Abrahamic religions.

Contrary to Christian belief, several liberal movements within Islam generally accept the scientific positions on the age of the earth, the age of the universe and evolution.

Islam also has its own school of theistic evolutionism in which they believe that scientific analysis of the origin of the universe is actually supported by the Qur'an. Many Muslims believe in evolutionary creationism, especially among liberal movements within Islam, although not all of them agree that one species can develop from another.

Islam: The universe is continually expanding.

The movement of Islamic creationism is growing. Similar to Christian creationism, there's concern regarding the conflicts between the Qur'an and evolution. Several verses in the Qur'an are compatible with the expansion of the universe, theories like the Big Bang and Big Crunch (an end-time self implosion of the earth), that is, that the universe has expanded from a primordial condition at some time in the past and continues to expand to this day. Among those verses are these:

"Do not the Unbelievers see that the skies (space) and the earth were joined together, then We clove them asunder and We created every living thing out of the water. Will they not then believe?" [Qur'an 21:30]

"Then turned He to the sky (space) when it was smoke, and said unto it and unto the earth: Come both of you, willingly or loth. They said: We come, obedient." [Qur'an 41:11]

"And it is We who have constructed the sky (space) with might, and it is We who are steadily expanding it." [Qur'an 51:47]

"On the day when We will roll up the sky (space) like the rolling up of the scroll for writings, as We originated the first creation, (so) We shall reproduce it; a promise (binding on Us); surely We will bring it about." [Qur'an 21:104]

In "Judaic creationism," Jews have differing views about creation, too, about the origin of life and the role of evolution in the formation of species. The major Jewish denominations, including many Orthodox Jewish groups, accept evolutionary creationism or theistic evolution. Conservative Judaism however, finds science a "challenge to traditional Jewish theology." That's probably what we'd expect.

───────── ✿ ─────────
Judiasm: The Torah can't be judged by scientific means.
───────── ✿ ─────────

Reform Judaism doesn't take the Torah as a literal text, but rather as a symbolic or open-ended work.

For Orthodox Jews, the notion that science and the Bible should even be subject to examination by traditional scientific means is uncomfortable at the least. If science is as true as the Torah, and if there seems to be a problem, our own limits in human knowledge are to blame for any apparent irreconcilable point. Things are not always as they appear. Just as Jews believe God created man and trees and the light on its way from the stars in their adult state, so too can they believe that the world was created in its adult state. The truth is, there are, and can be, no physical ways to verify any of this.

From those same Jewish Scriptures, we read in Isaiah 55:8, where God says, *"'My thoughts are nothing like your thoughts,' says the LORD. 'And my ways are far beyond anything you could imagine"* (New Living Translation).[1] That settles a lot of so-called discrepancies for Jews and for many of us. It sure does for me!

"Scientific critique" is a way of understanding one difference from another, using empirical evidence and testable explanations. Again, think back to our science classes in school. Natural causes can be reproduced and tested by scientists. But, explanations based on forces outside nature, like supernatural intervention, can't be confirmed or disproved by scientists because these explanations can't be tested.

Harvard University professor Stephen Jay Gould, a biologist and evolution teacher, postulated his theory of "punctuated equilibrium" which considered science and religion to be two compatible complementary fields which don't overlap. Since some claims of creationism can't be evaluated by science, such as the idea of a divine being as a first cause, the bottom line is it's simply not feasible to attempt to teach creationism as science, he said.

So, Which Theology Is Right?

Creationism is a difficult topic to study, because there are so many, many, complicated versions of theories. Still, those who believe in a God who can forgive sin and save a person from eternal hell, have no problem believing that God is the sole Creator of everything.

Theories are just that, mere propositions attempting to explain something which is still just guesstimated. Theories aren't science because they're not based on actual fact. They're really just contemplation, speculation, conjecture, propositions or, OK, just educated guesses. Theories are simply what different thinkers think. Therefore the best that we can take from such a study are questions to think about.

And guess what happens then?

We have more theories!

Evolution's not a scientific fact. It's a "belief system" about the past. We can't test the past using the scientific method of repeating things and watching them happen, since all evidence we have is in the present. Evolution, therefore, can only describe the way some folks *think* the evidence came to be here, now, in its present state.

God was there.

Creationism is also a belief about the past which describes the way in which the evidence in the present came to be, except in creationism, we Christians base our understanding on the Word of God.

God, who knows everything there is to know about everything,

God, who was there and

God, who is able to tell us what really happened.

So, in the final analysis, creationism is the account of God...

...God, who was there.

God dictated the origins of life to be written by Moses. Moses was God's appointed and God-blessed writer of the account.

Evolution attempts to be written by scientists, with various theories, by men who were not there.

So, this whole issue of *"Where did man start?"* revolves around whether we believe

the words of God who was there, or

the words of men who were not there.

We know by experience, that the Christian has become, by the grace of God, a "new creation" (II Corinthians 5:17 and Galatians 6:15) and "by faith" we understand *"that the worlds were framed by the word of God"* (Hebrews 11:3 and Revelation 4:11).

The inexperienced, the unbeliever, and in some cases the scientist, is in *"darkness"* (Psalms 107:10 and John 12:46) and *"receiveth not the things of the spirit of God...neither can he know them because they are spiritually discerned* (I Corinthians 2:14 and Romans 8:5)." They can't see spiritual things with natural eyes, no matter how educated they are.

What is at issue then, is our basic faith-commitment, and not so much the "raw" data of science, important as that is to accurately understand man's commission to subdue the earth as it says in Genesis 1:26-28. Faith inevitably determines the Christian's outlook on reality and influences his interpretation of so-called scientific facts.

"In the beginning, God..."
Genesis 1:1

Just as the Jesus limited himself by taking human form and dying on the cross, God limits His divine action in the world to be in accord with rational laws God has chosen. This enables you and me to understand the world on its own terms, but it also means that we surely still see through rose-colored glasses. And, that's the way God wants it.

And, that's good enough for me.

One final "creationism" thought: Genesis begins, *"In the beginning God created..."* Which is more important, the *'beginning"* part or the *"created"* part? The Bible tells us that for a person to see God, he must be born of "water" and of "spirit." We may be concerned with the water part because we live in the world, but that spirit part is really where our heart beats. Once born of the spirit of the God who created us, like the old song says, we Christians *"just can't feel at home in this world anymore..."*

For example, it doesn't take a very detailed scientific study to determine that basketball players are taller these days. Is that because we are evolving from Neanderthal Man or is it because basketball is more popular around the world and we're just finding more seven-footers now who can play the game? Yeah, it's a silly analogy. But, hey, it's a theory. There ya go.

Though one might be willing to accept the theory of theistic evolution as plausible inasmuch as it is still God-led, no evolution theories daunt my steadfast belief that God did in fact, create something out of nothing. Creationism really boils down to a belief in the Bible record as dictated by God Himself. God was there. Therefore, His account is accurate and unchangeable. Any other theory is not based on an eye-witness testimony, and at best, must include the jot and tittle of the Genesis account.

God's the originator of all physical and spiritual reality (John 1:3). He is Himself an non-created being and has a non-derived existence, independent from and above His creation (Psalms 90:2). Of that, there can be no argument.

God is my Creator. I am His servant.

And, I'm very happy in that.

---

[1] *State v. Scopes, Scopes v. State, 152 Tenn. 424, 278 S.W. 57 (Tenn. 1926)*

[2] Taylor, John H., *St. Augustine: The Literal Meaning of Genesis, Volume 1,* Ancient Christian Writers Series (Paulist Press, 1982)

3. Forster, Roger and Marston, Dr. Paul, "Chapter 7 - Genesis Through History", *Reason Science and Faith*, (Chester, England: Monarch Books, 2001) ISBN 1854244418.

4. Kenyon, Dean H. and Davis, Percival, *Of Pandas and People: The Central Question of Biological Origins* (Haughton Publishing Company, 1989)

5. Dembski, William and Wells, Jonathan, *The Design of Life: Discovering Signs of Intelligence in Biological Systems* (Foundation for Thought and Ethics; first edition, November 2007)

6. Mu, David, "Trojan Horse or Legitimate Science: Deconstructing the Debate over Intelligent Design," H*arvard Science Review,* Volume 19, Issue 1, Fall 2005.

7. *Tammy Kitzmiller, et al. v. Dover Area School District, et al.,* Case No. 04cv2688, in September, 2005, was the first direct challenge brought in the United States federal courts against a public school district that required the presentation of intelligent design as an alternative to evolution as an "explanation of the origin of life." The plaintiffs were represented by the ACLU.

8. Scott, Eugene and Eldridge, Niles, *Evolution Vs. Creationism* (University of California Press, 2005), pg. xxii.

9. Gosse, Philip Henry, *Omphalos: An Attempt to Untie the Geological Knot* (London: J. Van Voorst, 1857)

XII. Walk to the Future

Eschatology - All good things come to an end

Preface

"How will it all end?"

Eschatology. 'Big word, but pastors love it, so we should talk about it. Eschatology (pronounced "es-ka-tol'-ogy") is a study of future and final events, or "end times" as it were, as well as a study of the ultimate purpose of the world, of life, of humankind, and the church. So that's a bunch. But how exciting!

Christian eschatology concerns the establishment of the Kingdom of God, and the consummation of all of God's purposes, the fulfillment of Messianic prophecy and the beginning of the Messianic Age.

In his Epistle to the Romans, Paul wrote: *"We know that the whole creation has been groaning together in the pains of childbirth until now. And not only the creation, but we ourselves, who have the first fruits of the Spirit, groan inwardly as we wait eagerly for adoption as sons, the redemption of our bodies.*

"In this hope we were saved. Now hope that is seen is not hope. For who hopes for what he sees? But if we hope for what we do not see, we wait for it with patience" (Romans 8:19).

> *"Study the past if you would define the future."*
> Confucius

So we wait. For something we've not seen. In the meantime, it's helpful to understand eschatology, and examine death, Heaven and the New Earth to come, and its counterpart, Hell. At the same time, let's look at Christian eschatology, the return of Jesus, the resurrection of the dead, the judgment and the time when all that will all happen. All this will help us in our Walk With God today.

The major views of "end times" include amillennialism, premillennialism, postmillennialism and dispensationalism. Don't worry about the 50-cent words. We'll get to them.

The term "eschatology" is often used in a more popular and narrower sense when comparing various interpretations of the Book of Revelation and other prophesy parts of the Bible. These include the Old Testament Book of Daniel and some various sayings of Jesus in the New Testament, such as the *"Olivet Discourse"* (on the "end times") and the *"Judgment of the Nations,"* concerning the timing of His imminent second coming. The thinkers think differently when it comes to the order of events leading to, and following the return of Jesus and the religious significance of these events.

Understanding the basics of eschatology will help us live our lives, because it'll shape what we expect to occur in God's plan. Let's start with some basic foundations:

Death

What a place to start, huh? Death. Well, when you stop to think about it, while the Christian at conversion is blessed with an anticipation of a *life* with our Savior, at the same time, we become much more aware of *death*. Since the sin of Adam, the Bible talks a lot about death. The body, created of dust, returns to dust (Genesis 3:19) and no one is exempt from death (Romans 5:12). Moreover, the wages of sin is death (Romans 6:23).

> *"Momma always said dyin' was a part of life."*
> Forest Gump

But, for the Christian, the physical death is not such a big deal. The stories of Lazarus and the rich man (Luke 16:22-23) describe their existence after death, one in "Abraham's bosom," the other in torment of Hell. Paul tells us that death just means to *"be absent from the body and to be at home with the Lord* (II Corinthians 5:8)." That's actually a very good thing. For the Christian, to die is gain (Philippians 1:21).

Jesus Did It All...

...all to Him I owe, sin had left a crimson stain, but He washed it white as snow.

Through Jesus' death and resurrection, He destroyed the power of death. Man, who once feared death, should fear it no more. We can stand on Jesus' promise, *"I am the resurrection and the life. He who believes in me will live even if he dies. Everyone who lives in me will never die"* (John 11:25-26).

God created us in His image, a spirit, and the spirit part of us will live with Him eternally. That spirit in us will never die. The Bible tells us so: *"The dust will return to the earth as it was, and the spirit will return to God who gave it"* (Ecclesiastes 12:7). Jesus conquered death. Believers will be immortal (I Corinthians 15.53), in a new body.

In his book, *"The Moody Handbook of Theology,"* Paul Enns creates a beautiful picture of the welcome in Heaven. Paul says that when the Sanhedrin had Stephen stoned to death, as told in the seventh chapter of Acts, Stephen *"gazed intently into heaven and saw the glory of God, and Jesus standing at the right hand of God."*[1] In Hebrews, Jesus is seated at the right hand of the Father in Heaven, *"but at the believer's death,"* Paul writes, *"Jesus rises from His seat and stands to welcome His servant into heaven!"*

Jesus gave a magnanimous reward to the thief on the cross, when He told him, *"Truly I say to you, today you'll be with me in Paradise"* (Luke 23:43). And, the thief's role in earning that lofty gift? Well, let's see: He never went to Sunday School. He never sat in church. He never sang a song, heard a sermon or encountered a Roman Road of Scriptures. He never said a sinner's prayer or walked an aisle or joined a church and he was never baptized. What he did do was call Jesus, *"Lord."* With that one word, and a sincere heart, he recognized Jesus as God's Son. And, obviously he meant it. The ultimate of "end times" is Heaven, and Heaven is the immediate destination of everyone who knows Jesus as *Lord*.

Look at this: In John 14, Jesus tells us, *"Let not your heart be troubled: ye believe in God, believe also in me. In my Father's house are many mansions: if it were not so, I would have told you. I go to prepare a place for you. And if I go and prepare a place for you, I will come again, and receive you unto myself; that where I am, there ye may be also."* We're all going to die. Forest Gump's momma told us that. And it's a rule: if it's in the movies, it has to be true, right? But how comforting is it, that at the very moment of taking our last earthly breath, Jesus will come, take us literally by the hand, and personally usher us to Heaven! That's the work of a Best Friend. I don't even have to know the way to Heaven. Jesus says, *"You know where I am going, and you know the way"* (John 14:4 NIV). Jesus is the Way!

Heaven

Heaven is an awesome place. Revelation 21:18-21 tells us of streets of gold and walls of jasper in Heaven. Did you know that jasper are semi-precious stones? They are an opaque, cryptocrystalline variety of quartz. They are translucent, so light is able to pass through them. Therefore, from these jasper walls, brilliant rays of dazzling color radiate for all to see. That's gotta be awesome! The glory of the city will be visible from afar, and even those outside the walls will behold its brightness. Wow!

Although the wall around the city is real, it's also symbolic. The purpose of the wall is not to preserve the city against invaders, for God will have no enemies in Heaven. Being 216 feet high, it impressively signifies that no one will enter the city apart from God's grace. The wall's too high to be scaled by human effort, and the only portals are the 12 guarded gates. The requirement for admittance is salvation, and no one who has rejected God's plan will be able to go in. They can *see* in, but they can't get there!

The next thing to catch our vision as we look at the city is its jeweled foundation. I believe that these jewels reflect all the colors of the rainbow, though we do not know the precise characteristics of each stone. Beginning at ground level, these were the colors seen by the apostle John in Revelation 21:

> The jasper stone may have been a light green or yellow;
>
> The sapphire, a sky-blue or azure;
>
> The chalcedony, containing a combination of colors, was mostly green and blue;
>
> The emerald is of course, bright green;
>
> The sardonyx, red and white;
>
> The sardius, reddish in color;
>
> Chrysolite, golden yellow;
>
> Beryl, sea-green;
>
> Topaz, yellow-green and transparent;
>
> Chrysoprasus, golden-green;
>
> Jacinth, violet; and
>
> Amethyst, either rose-red or purple.

The radiating light of the city, shining out through the jasper wall and blazing through the open gates, reflects from these precious stones in splendorous color. What a dazzling place!

The street of the city is pure gold, like transparent glass (Revelation 21:12, 21). In fact, one of the characteristics of the heavenly city is the abundance of gold. A precious commodity throughout man's history, gold has been used as an overlay in works of art and as a standard of value, and has been the means of a great amount of both good and evil in society. Gold served the purposes of God in the tabernacle and temple, for much gold was in evidence there.

Today, at St. Peter's Basilica in Rome, people worship in what is called "the greatest of all churches of Christendom" with walls laden with gold, enough gold perhaps to feed the world, as postulated in the 1968 movie, "*Shoes of the Fisherman*."

Gold, of course, was also used by idolaters in the making of images.

On Earth, men have fought, suffered and died for it, but in Heaven, gold will be so plentiful that it will be used for cobblestones and building blocks. It'll be like glass, possessing transparent qualities, so that the glorious light of the Holy City will both shine through it and be reflected by it. Here is John's description: *"The city was pure gold, like clear glass...and the street of the city was pure gold, like transparent glass"* (Revelation 21:18,21).

Traditionally, gold has symbolized purity. At a marriage, the wedding band, given and taken, is a circle of gold. It speaks of endlessness and the gold stands for purity. The golden street of Heaven, therefore, might well suggest a pure and holy "Walk With God" by His redeemed in eternal paradise. Can't you just see it? The brightness of the city, reflecting from the gold that abounds everywhere, will have its uncorrupted counterpart within the heart of every citizen of Heaven. Purity pervades the eternal Paradise of God! What a reward!

Purity Pervades the Paradise of God!

Take me there, Lord! Let me Walk With God!

Some Bible scholars believe that the gates of pearl are a beautiful picture of salvation by grace. Even as a wound to an oyster results in the formation of a valuable pearl, the gates of Heaven can be entered only because the Lord Jesus was *"wounded for our transgressions"* (Isaiah 53:5). That's a pure one-on-one! Although men wickedly rejected Him and crucified Him, it was through this death that salvation was made possible. Now, all who believe on Him can look forward to entering the pearly gates of Heaven. Jesus Himself said, *"I am the door. If anyone enters by Me, he will be saved"* (John 10:9).

The gates are open at all times and in every direction, for salvation is still offered freely to everyone. The angels who keep watch at the open gates, therefore, are a wonderful contrast to the cherubim who guarded the closed gate of Eden after Adam and Eve sinned. These angels keep the way of access open, while the cherubim kept the Garden closed to fallen humanity.

A river, clear as crystal, will flow through Heaven. The apostle John declared, *"And he showed me a pure river of water of life, clear as crystal, proceeding from the throne of God and of the Lamb"* (Revelation 22:1). Just as in Eden there was a river to water the garden, so also in Heaven

Walk to the Future

there will be a river of life. It'll begin at the throne of God, the very uppermost part of the city, and it'll course downward through all of Heaven. In Heaven, the river of crystal will flow forever, reminding us for all eternity that God has graciously and abundantly provided for our every spiritual need. Remember, life in Heaven will not be a nebulous existence in some nameless place. No indeed! We'll lead rich and full lives in glorified bodies. We'll dwell in a real city of gold, and our lives will be filled with significance and meaning as we give praise to our Redeemer and gladly do His bidding.

This crystal river flowing through our eternal home will be of sparkling beauty and of clarity beyond the purest water a person has ever seen. Think of it! All who believe in Christ will walk the banks of this glorious crystal river. What a joy will then be ours!

It's difficult to envision just how the trees, the crystal river and the street of gold will be related. Some teachers feel that a river will flow through the middle of a broad street, and that alongside the river on each bank will be the trees. Others believe that a grove of trees, including the Tree of Life, is centered between the avenue of gold on one side and the river on the other. Regardless of which

Being in God's presence will bring an intensity of delight that will far exceed Earth.

view, it's evident that those who conceive of Heaven as a place where the redeemed will do nothing but sit on golden stairs playing harps are grossly mistaken. Life in Heaven will be filled with beauty and variety. It'll be, how shall we say it... heavenly!

Heaven is prepared for us by God (I Corinthians 2:9). There, no pain, no death, no sadness, no sorrow, no sickness or poverty exists (Revelation 21:3-4). Being in God's presence will bring an intensity of delight that will far exceed Earth (John 15:11). We will function as the person we are (Revelation 4:10-11). Our real self will live on in Heaven, not some other being. God made you to be you. We are His Workmanship and to reject that is to be like the unprofitable servant who hid his master's talent in the ground.

Furthermore, we'll judge angels (I Corinthians 6:3).

We'll see our blessed Mama again (Luke 23:42-43, Hebrews 12:22-23). The "specialness" of our loved ones won't be removed, nor will the reasons why we love them. That's part of who we are. Indeed, anything which mediates God's Goodness and God's Love will be there - including Fluffy, my granddaughter's pet. At the very least, the *love* of Fluffy will be manifested, for sure. The Bible tells us God is love (I John 4:16). Billy Graham once said, *"God will prepare everything for our perfect happiness in heaven, and if it takes my dog being there, I believe he'll be there."* Don't you just love Billy Graham?

There will be no past and no regrets. There will be no future and no fears. There will be no sin because we will not want to sin, nor will there be an influence to sin. God and sin can't exist in the same place. Can you imagine a place completely free from sin? Wow!

Revelation 21:1 tells us of *"a new Heaven [sky] and a new Earth"* in the end times. Whatever the dispensation, Heaven is a new place. There is no sun and moon, therefore, no gravity. Heavenly bodies will wear no clothes, nothing to hide, no shame. It's a place where the *"woman [is] clothed with the sun* (Rev. 12:1)." Everything in pure harmony, possibly even musically inaudible. There is no age, no one is immature, no one is old, and everyone will communicate in one language. There'll be no misunderstanding in Heaven.

Earth

As for this place down here, remember that when God completed His creating, He called what He'd created *"very good."* The fact is, in the days of Adam, it was more than very good, it was perfect. God would not allow Satan and his antichrist to lead mankind to oblivion, causing God to destroy the world which He designed as "very good" and thus hand Satan a victory. Even in the time of Noah, mankind was preserved. No, Satan will be cast into the Lake of Fire, and Earth as we know it, will be destroyed on the surface by fire, but replaced with a New Heaven and a New Earth, which will be magnificent.

This fire is the judgment of incorrigible sinners, the Lake of Fire

(Revelation 20:14). In this unquenchable fire, the unrepentant will completely burn up (Matthew 3:10-12). Peter tells us the effects of this unquenchable fire will be a great noise, a fervent heat that can't be extinguished. All the earth and everything in it will be burned up. Just as the earth continued to exist after the Flood, so Earth will continue to exist after the coming worldwide "Gehenna" fire (Matthew 5:29-30; 10:28), but the surface of the earth and everything physical on it, including the incorrigible wicked, will be destroyed by the all-consuming fire. God will then renew the earth's surface (the New Earth). Psalm 104:30 prophesies that this will happen. It says of God, *"When you give them your breath, life is created, and you renew the face of the earth."*

God will make the New Earth a pure, glorious habitation for Himself and the rest of the God Kingdom. John in Revelation 21:1 says, *"And I saw a new heaven and a new earth: for the first heaven and the first earth were passed away; and there was no more sea."*

Louis Talbot, once a preacher in nearby Paris, Texas, said, *"The new earth will emerge from that baptism of elemental and judicial fire, clean, beautiful, holy. Every stain of sin, every mark of evil, will be wiped out. The condition of the earth as it was according to the record of Genesis 1:1 will be restored with a plus."*[2]

So, what will happen to the righteous?

After the millennium and the final judgment, the Bride of Christ, that is those who are saved, will live in the New Earth and New Jerusalem (prophesied by Isaiah 65:17 and 66:22). Since there will be no more sea, the increased land space will be fully capable of handling large numbers of redeemed people from all ages.

God will dwell with man, says Revelation 21:3.

There will be no more tears, death, sorrow, crying, or pain. Watch this: This is the exact opposite of the curse that resulted from Adam's sin. In other words, John 3:16 ushers in Genesis 3:16). How awesome is that?

So, what will happen to the un-righteous?

Revelation 21:8 tells us, *"But the fearful, and unbelieving, and the abominable, and murderers, and whoremongers, and sorcerers, and* idolaters, and all liars, shall have their part in the lake which burneth with fire and brimstone: which is the second death."

Is that the way God wants it? No! God is *"not willing that any should perish, but that all should come to repentance* (II Peter 3:9)." So, Christians, Peter tells us that we have a spiritual and moral obligation, as sons of God and Children of the Savior, to live holy lifestyles, repentant and sold out to the Lord.

Hell

In the Old Testament, the word translated "Hell" is *Sheol*, in the New Testament, it's *Hades* (meaning "unseen") and *Gehenna* ("the Valley of Hinnom") and *Hell*. *Sheol* is also translated as "pit" and "grave."

Both Sheol and Hades refer to a temporary abode of the dead before judgment (Psalm 9:17; Revelation 1:18). Gehenna refers to an eternal state of punishment for the wicked dead (Mark 9:43).

> *According to the Bible, Hell is just as real as Heaven.*

According to the Bible, Hell is just as real as Heaven. The Bible clearly and explicitly teaches that Hell is a real place to which the unbelievers are sent after death. We've all sinned against God and fallen short of the glory for which he designed us (Romans 3:23). Understand, of course, that all of our sin is ultimately against God (Psalm 51:4).

The just punishment for that sin and shortcoming is death (Romans 6:23). Since God is an infinite and eternal Being, the punishment for sin, that is, death, must also be infinite and eternal. Hell is this infinite and eternal death which we have earned because of our sin.

The punishment of the wicked in Hell is described throughout Scripture, as *"eternal fire"* (Matthew 25:41), *"unquenchable fire"* (Matthew 3:12), *"shame and everlasting contempt"* (Daniel 12:2), a place where *"the fire is not quenched"* (Mark 9:44-49), a place of *"torment"* and *"fire"* (Luke 16:23-24), *"everlasting destruction"* (II Thessalonians 1:9), where *"the smoke of torment rises forever and ever"* (Revelation 14:10-11), and a *"lake of burning sulfur"* where the wicked are *"tormented day and night forever and ever"* (Revelation 20:10).

No doubt, Hell's a very nasty place.

Worse, the punishment has no end. Jesus Himself indicates that punishment in Hell is just as everlasting as life in Heaven (Matthew 25:46). The wicked are forever subject to the fury and the wrath of God. Those in Hell will acknowledge the perfect justice of God (Psalm 76:10). They'll know that their punishment is just and that they alone are to blame (Deuteronomy 32:3-5). Praise Jesus, I've escaped this eternal fate (John 3:16, 18, 36)! I truly hope you have, too!

While Jews deny that Hell exists and Universalists believe all will ultimately be saved from Hell, Seventh Day Adventists and Jehovah's witnesses believe in the ultimate annihilation of the wicked. Ellen White, the so-called prophet of the Seventh Day Adventists, professed that the wicked will burn in proportion to their sins. Ranking sins? What could be more serious than original sin?

Salvation will be reserved for those who have accepted Jesus as Savior. Jesus said, "No man comes to the Father but by me" (John 14:6) and "Neither is there salvation in any other" (Acts 4:12). Outside of the gospel, there is no salvation from Hell. The Bible never says that there are degrees of punishment. Hell is hell. It is everlasting, literal and real.

Don't be fooled into thinking otherwise.

The Return of Jesus and the Resurrection

More than a hundred times, God's Word tells us that Jesus will return in a Second Coming, a literal, physical event. Moreover, Jesus tells us that his return will bring us comfort. In John 14, Jesus tells us not to be troubled, that He's already at work preparing our Heavenly home and that He'll come again and take us there. Those whom Jesus knows will rise from the dead, receiving new immortal bodies (I Thessalonians 4:13-18).

Jesus rebuked the Sadducees because they didn't understand the resurrection of the dead. That's why the Sadducees were "sad, you see." They didn't understand the Scriptures, for the Old Testament clearly taught about the resurrection. Neither did they really understand the power of God, who is able to raise the dead. Jesus spoke words reminiscent of Daniel when He explained that the dead would hear His voice and come forth, some to a resurrection life and some to a resurrection judgment. He reassured his believers that He will raise us from the dead in John 6:39-40, 44 and 54. He demonstrated that at the raising of Lazarus, and told us all that if we believe in Him, we will never die.

Life after Death

Most Christian traditions preach that a belief in life after death is a central part of the faith. Belief in an afterlife was already prevalent in Jewish thinking among the Pharisees and Essenes even before Christ's resurrection. When the Sadducees were testing him, Jesus explained that God is the God of the living, not of the dead, yet He spoke of God as the God of Abraham and Isaac and Jacob, three apparently dead people wouldn't you say? In Matthew 22:31, Jesus said, *"But about the resurrection of the dead, have you not read what God said to you, 'I am the God of Abraham, the God of Isaac, and the God of Jacob?' He is not the God of the dead but of the living."*

The dead alive? Yes. What does Jesus know that we're still learning?

God's servant, Job, said, *"And after my skin has been destroyed, yet in my flesh I will see God; I myself will see him with my own eyes. I, and not another"* (Job 19:26). Pretty smart guy, Job. In his opinion, though he should die, he never would at any point cease to exist. Nor would he at any point be unreachable, that is "dead" to God. In Job 14, he explains, *"But man dies, and is laid low; man breathes his last, and where is he? As waters fall from a lake, and a river wastes away and dries up, so man lies down and rises not again; till the heavens are no more he will not awake, or be aroused out of his sleep."*

The Roman Catholic church believes in a place called "Purgatory," an interim location where the souls of those who have died in a state of grace are believed to undergo a limited amount of suffering to expiate their venial (lesser, forgivable) sins and become purified of the remaining effects of mortal sin. The concept or mention of Purgatory is simply nowhere in the Bible. Jesus spoke significantly of both Heaven and Hell, but He never mentioned a third place. More important, the idea of purgatory implies that Christ's work on the cross was incomplete and insufficient by itself to save us from judgment for our sins. No, the full redemptive work of Christ was accomplished on the cross, just as Christ Himself declared, *"It is finished"* (John 19:30). It was and it is.

> *The concept or mention of Purgatory is simply nowhere in the Bible.*

For believers, the end of this life will be the beginning of our eternal life with the Lord. Same day. Same moment! We can see this in Jesus' story about the rich man and Lazarus. Lazarus was taken (by Jesus) immediately upon his death to "Abraham's side," a common figure-of-speech for Heaven. The rich man was immediately cast into torment in Hades. The Bible tells us: *"When the Son of Man comes in his glory, and all the angels with him, then he will sit on his glorious throne. Before him will be gathered all the nations, and he will separate people one from another as a shepherd separates the sheep from the goats. And he will place the sheep on his right, but the goats on the left. Then the King will say to those on his right, 'Come, you who are blessed by my Father, inherit the kingdom prepared for you from the foundation of the world'"* (Matthew 25:31-34 ESV).

> *For believers, the end of this life will be the beginning of our eternal life with the Lord.*

John Calvin included this belief among those things not worth arguing about. Later Protestants also rejected any idea of an intervening experience for the soul after death, prior to being in the presence of God. That includes purgatory.

However, the Catholic and Orthodox faiths are united against the Protestants in their doctrine that the souls of at least some of the saints in Heaven are aware of those who call upon them in request of their intercession. That's nonsense. Souls of those who have died neither could or should be called upon for help or intercession with God. When you can pray directly to God, why would you want to pray to the dead? Prayers directed toward those who have died, or rituals or masses dedicated to assisting the dead in their salvation, are just flat contrary to Scripture. There's no evidence that souls of people who die adopt any kind of omniscience, omnipresence or ubiquity after death, or that they're troubled any longer with the trials of life, or that their virtue in a new life can benefit the Church or the living down here in any way. Uncle Charlie can't help you Walk With God, if he's already gone to his reward!

The Judgment

Because God is Holy, he must judge all that is unholy, or else He would no longer be holy. That makes sense, doesn't it?

Jesus announced a future judgment connected with His return when He said people would be judged according to their deeds (Matthew 16:27). At the Great White Throne Judgment, all will be found guilty and unworthy of eternal life. Thank God, there's more! There's Jesus!

The return of Jesus is the most important eschatological event of all.

So then, the eternal question is, where will you be sitting in eternity, smoking or non-smoking? God, in the Person of His Son, offers us a clear choice.

The Second Coming

As Paul explained, eschatology concerns the things hoped for, yet to be revealed (Hebrews 1:11). The return of Jesus Christ is the most important and most hopeful eschatological (end times) event of all. Jesus told the apostles at the Last Supper, *"I have earnestly desired to eat this Passover with you before I suffer. For I tell you I will not eat it until it is fulfilled in the kingdom of God. For as often as you eat this bread and drink the cup, you proclaim the Lord's death until he comes"* (Luke 22:15).

With the Second Coming of Christ, we Christians anticipate a resurrection of both the righteous and the wicked. The last enemy, death, will be vanquished. When Jesus comes, the dead in Christ are going to be raised from their resting place.

The saved will be changed into heavenly bodies, immortal bodies, and they will be taken up in the rapture.

The wicked dead will be raised but they will not be changed. They will be in the same state as when they died, in mortal bodies.

Following the resurrection of the dead, Christ will personally judge the living and the dead, to determine the eternal destiny of each according to whether their names are written in the Lamb's Book of Life.

What Will Happen and When?

Don't let these big words intimidate you, but in "end times" theology, there are four major views concerning future and the end times, or last things:

        dispensational premillennialism,
        historic premillennialism,
        amillennialism and
        postmillennialism.

They all relate to a millennium or a "thousand-year reign" of Christ, stemming from the Scripture in Revelation 20:4, *"They came to life and reigned with Christ for a thousand years."*

The theological question is: Should this Scripture be taken literally or symbolically? Read on.

"Premillennial" views include the belief that the millennium is a *future* event and Jesus will return *before* His 1,000-year reign as described in Revelation 20:4.

The "amillennial" view considers that the millennium is a symbol of Christ's *present* reign among His people.

"Postmillennialists" believe that Jesus will return *after* the 1,000-year reign. The millennium itself is a time when most of the world submits to Jesus, and peace and justice reign. Sound like today? Hmmm.

Dispensational Premillennialism

"Dispensational Premillennialism" is not as difficult to understand as the complicated words might intimate.

Dispensational premillennialists believe that Jesus:
> will come back to earth after a 7-year tribulation and
> will rule during a 1000-year time of peace on Earth.

God will still give Israel the land from the river of Egypt (Nile) to the river Euphrates (in Iraq), the full extent of King Solomon's kingdom (Genesis 15:18). That includes the West Bank, Gaza, Palestine and probably parts of Turkey, Lebanon, Syria, Iraq, Jordan, Egypt and the Sinai Peninsula. That's a lot of land!

The Dispensations

First, let's look at the "dispensation" part. It's easy. This view separates all of history into seven dispensations or periods of time:

The age of Innocence (Genesis 1:1–3:7), prior to Adam's fall, covers basically
> man's state,
> his responsibility and his failure, and of course
> the consequences of that failure (the Fall).

The age of Conscience (Genesis 3:8–8:22), Adam to Noah, includes the
> line of Cain, and the
> line of Seth who was the ancestor to the
> line of mankind. It spanned 1,656 years.

Walk to the Future

The age called Civil Government (Genesis 9:1–11:32), Noah to Abraham, spans 426 years, and covers the time of
> Noah and his three sons, Shem, Ham and Japheth,
> the wickedness of the world and
> the Flood, and
> the beginning of the repopulation of the earth into nations, thus the name.

The age of Promise or Patriarchal Rule (Genesis 12:1–Exodus 19:25), Abraham to Moses, about 430 years, includes
> the call of Abram, and Lot, and
> the establishment of Israel with the Covenant of Abraham.
> Of course, it was through Israel that God sent Jesus, our Messiah, Savior and Lord.

The age of the Law (Exodus 20:1–Acts 2:4), Moses to Christ, about 1524 years, includes
> the history from the time of Moses and Elijah, through
> the captives in Assyria in 722 BC and in Babylon in 597 BC,
> the influence of Persia and Greece and
> the dominance of Rome.

The age of Grace-Church (Acts 2:4–Revelation 20:3) is the age of today. It began 50 days after Christ's death on the cross (Pentecost) and includes
> the life and death of our Savior Jesus Christ, and His resurrection and Christ's ascent in Acts 1:9.
> Christ will come one day, like a thief in the night, to rapture the church before the seven-year Tribulation ("pre-Trib"), a time of judgment on the earth.

The Millennial Kingdom (Revelation 20:4–20:6). This is the Age to Come.
> After the Tribulation,
> Christ will return to reign in His Millennial Kingdom.

Dispensationalists believe that God has yet to fulfill his promises to national Israel, including:
> the land promises,

> a millennial kingdom,
>
> a Third Temple, perhaps in place of the Muslims' Al Aqsa Mosque which occupies the primary real estate of today's Temple Mount, where it's been since 705 AD.

Secondly, Christ, upon his return, will rule the world from Jerusalem, so a good question would be what modifications will effect the "four quarters" layout of Jerusalem today, the

> Jewish quarter,
> Muslim quarter,
> Armenian quarter and
> Christian quarter?

We can only wonder.

During the Tribulation, wars and disasters will occur and suffering will take place.

> Many Jews will turn to Jesus.
>
> All prophesies in Revelation will come true.

After the Tribulation, Jesus will return and reign over a 1,000-year millennium of peace on Earth.

When will the tribulation happen?

After the 1,000 years, the Final Judgment takes place and the world ends. God will create a new Heaven and a New Earth.

Most dispensational premillennialists are pre-tribulation. That would make them dispensational premillennial pretribulationists. (OK, close your eyes and spell that.)

They believe that the church will be "raptured" (Revelation 4:1-2; I Thessalonians 4:13-18) *prior* to the tribulation period ("pre-trib").

God will judge unbelievers *during* the tribulation.

At the *end* of the tribulation, Christ will return and establish the millennial kingdom on Earth.

Following the 1,000-year reign, Satan will be freed once more, whereupon he and his followers will be cast into the Lake of Fire as in Revelation 20, and Eternity will follow after that.

Some dispensational premillennialists are mid-tribulation. That would make them dispensational premillennial midtribulationists. They believe that the rapture will occur three-and-a-half years into the great tribulation, the half-way point ("mid-trib").

Dispensational premillennialism, then, can be defined by its two basic features:

> A distinction made between God's program for Israel and His program for the church, and,
>
> A consistently literal interpretation of the Scriptures.

As for the distinction between Israel and the church, the term Israel always refers to a distinct entity and there is no reason for changing that. Israel was given unconditional covenants by God which must be fulfilled in the millennial kingdom. The church, on the other hand, is also a distinct entity, born at Pentecost.

The foundations for dispensational premillennialism then are found in those Old Testament covenants with Israel, in the Scriptures. These covenants were "literal," unconditional and eternal. They include covenants with Adam and Eve, Noah, Abraham, Moses, David and the New Covenant with Jesus, and if you will, the covenant with Man upon our acceptance of Jesus as Lord. As other prophesies have been fulfilled in perfection, it is reasonable to believe that these must be also.

These include the Palestinian Covenant in Deuteronomy wherein Israel has eternal right to that land. Sorry, Palestinians. This Covenant is why a peace between Israel and Palestine is so difficult and so important, if not impossible before the Rapture!

It also includes the Davidic Covenant in II Samuel 7:12-16, which promises a kingdom of David's line forever. Jesus is from the Davidic Line.

Finally, it includes the new covenant in Jeremiah 31:31-34,

During the millennium, there will be peace, joy and comfort.

that provides the basis by which God will bless Israel in the future, forgiveness of sins through Christ.

It's not hard to argue that "literally" is the only right way to interpret Scriptures. Over many years, Scriptures have literally been fulfilled, just as they had been prophesied. Surely, they'll be fulfilled just like that in the future. The Bible tells us that to interpret Scripture any other way is to risk the wrath of God. Jesus counsels, *"For assuredly, I say to you, till heaven and earth pass away, one jot or one tittle will by no means pass from the law till all is fulfilled. Whoever therefore breaks one of the least of these commandments, and teaches men so, shall be called least in the kingdom of heaven"* (Matthew 5:18). Don't do that!

When Christ returns to Earth, He will establish Himself as King in Jerusalem, sitting on the throne of David (Luke 1:32-33). The unconditional covenants demand a literal and physical return of Jesus. During the millennium, there will be peace, joy and comfort. There will be no poverty or sickness. Because only believers will enter the millennium, obviously there will be truth and righteousness.

Won't it be nice to be able to inexplicably trust your neighbor, and even watch TV (if that will be an activity at all) and live in a world without the constant bombardment "in our face," of vile, sexual and sinful ugliness, fear and sadness? Eternity, the destination of all the redeemed, will begin. Praise God!

Today's dispensationalists include Charles Stanley, John Hagee, Tim LaHaye, Hal Lindsay, Chuck Swindoll and Charles Caldwell Ryrie.

Historic Premillennialism

In the end time view of "Historic Premillennialism," society grows increasingly evil. Some argue that's definitely happening today.

In Historic Premillennialism, Christians will remain on Earth during the Tribulation. As attractive as dispensational premillennialism is, the view of historic premillennialism is hard to ignore when we seem to be bombarded with tsunamis, wicked hurricanes and tornados, mass destructions, wars and rumors of wars, sex and hedonism rampant and even American socialism on a train-wreck course! Historic premillennialists believe that the tribulation will actually purify the churches by rooting out false believers, and the Second Coming of Christ will precede the millennium.

Historic premillennialism believes that the church has replaced

Walk to the Future

Israel as God's covenant people, therefore it is also known as "covenant premillennialism."

Historic premillennialism views one body of Christians of all ages, now revealed as the body of Christ. Thus, historic premillennialists believe that the church will indeed go through the Great Tribulation, and will not see a separate rapture beforehand, say believers in the dispensational system.

Historic premillennialists argue that:

> God's promises of land and blessings to Abraham and his offspring were conditional promises, based on their obedience. Israel's present disobedience has destroyed God's covenant with them. (The Scriptures are clear that God's covenant with Abraham was a totally unconditional one. No amount of disobedience can change that, as we've already seen. Surely, the Israelites of the Old Testament tested God on this matter many times over!)
>
> The "body of believers" who have trusted in God and His grace is the true Israel (Romans 9:6-8). Therefore, references to Israel in Revelation refer symbolically to all believers, the church, not just the nation of Israel as we know it today.
>
> The church on Earth during the Tribulation will experience suffering but not to the extent of the unbelievers;
>
> All are resurrected before Christ's kingdom is established;
>
> One second coming will occur where the marriage feast of the Lamb will take place and Christ will unite with His bride the church. It's an interesting footnote to realize that the marriage itself references the church and takes place in Heaven, while the marriage supper references Israel and takes place on Earth in the form of the millennial kingdom.[8]
>
> Christ will conquer His enemies, consigning the Beast and the False Prophet to the Lake of Fire (Revelation 19:20). The Devil will be bound in the bottomless pit for a thousand years, at the end of which he, too, will be cast into the Lake of Fire.

In historic premillennialism, Christ is reigning *now*, from Heaven.[9] In fact, Christ began His Messianic reign at his resurrection and ascension (a little less than 2,000 years ago), but His present reign is invisible. The order of the Age to Come will involve a New Heaven and a New Earth and will be so different from the present order that we can speak of it as beyond history.[10]

Modern supporters of historic millennialism include David Dockery and George E. Ladd.[11]

Amillennialism

"Amillennialists" believe that Jesus will come "some day," but there will be no literal 1,000-year rule on Earth.

Rather, they believe, the millennium symbolizes Christ's reign in the lives of Christians *today,* from the beginning of the Church until His Second Coming. They believe that the millennium and the tribulation are running *together now,* simultaneously. Persecution of Christians is occurring now (hard to argue) and will continue until the Second Coming, when

> Christ will defeat Satan,
> resurrect the saved and unsaved,
> judge them and
> deliver them to their eternal destinies (Heaven and Hell).
> The Second Coming of Christ and the resurrection of the saved and unsaved will occur at the same time.

Amillennialists believe that Christ triumphed over Satan at the Cross, and in doing so, Jesus restrained the power of Satan on Earth. *The tribulation is going on now* and persecution of Christians along with the expansion of the kingdom (the millennium) will continue to occur until Jesus returns.

Christ triumphed over Satan at the Cross.

The Second Coming will be a single event, where, like the dispensationalists believe, Christ's Second Coming will actually be accomplished in two phases. Amillennialists believe that certain events must be accomplished before Christ will return. These events include:

The evangelizing of all the world, the calling of the Gentiles. (Matthew 24:14, Mark 13:10, Romans 11:25);

The conversion of Israel (Romans 11:26);

The Great Apostasy (turning away from Christ) and the Great Tribulation (Matthew 24:9-12, 21-24, Mark 13:9-22) and Luke 21:22-24);[3]

The revealing of the Antichrist;

Signs and wonders, meaning wars, false prophets, astonishing satanic miracles and signs in the heavens.

The Bible tells us that no one knows when Christ will return. Paul tells us in I Thessalonians 5:2, that *"the day of the Lord so cometh as a thief in the night."* Christ's second coming will end the world. Eternity will begin. The dead, both believers and unbelievers, will be resurrected and the final judgment will be made.

All this differs with "premillennialism," which teaches that Christ's second coming is not the signal of the end of the world but a time when Jesus will establish His earthly thousand-year kingdom.

"Amillennialism" teaches that the body of a resurrected believer will be in a fundamental sense identical with his present body.[4]

The Bible tells us in Daniel 12:2-3: *"Many of those whose bodies lie dead and buried will rise up, some to everlasting life and some to shame and everlasting disgrace. Those who are wise will shine as bright as the sky, and those who lead many to righteousness will shine like the stars forever."*

John 5:28-29: *"Don't be so surprised! Indeed, the time is coming when all the dead in their graves will hear the voice of God's Son, and they will rise again. Those who have done good will rise to experience eternal life, and those who have continued in evil will rise to experience judgment."*

Postmillennialism

Finally, "postmillennialists" believe that the Second Coming will occur only when, through the preaching of the Gospel, *most of the world will come to Christ* as society gradually improves.

During the times we're in now, God has bound Satan who has no power. *Once the church attains full power,* then the church will usher in the thousand-year reign.

> The second coming will occur after the millennium.
>
> Christ will rule during the millennium, but Christ will not be physically present.
>
> Christ will return *after* the millennium.
>
> The present age will progress morally and spiritually until it brings about the millennial age with Jesus returning at the conclusion of the millennium. Got it?

During that time, Satan will have no power over the earth and evil regimes will collapse (Revelation 19:19-20:3). A period of great tribulation may precede the millennium. Charismatic Christians embrace *"dominion postmillennialism,"* which teaches that through the contemporary charismatic movement, God has been binding Satan.

Postmillennialists place great confidence in the preaching of the gospel, contending that the Gospel will eventually spread far and wide in a way that nearly everyone in the world will turn to Jesus, leading to a golden age. Sin will be present, although it'll be greatly reduced because of a great progress in the spreading of the Gospel. Most people will turn to Christ. Christian principles will be the norm in the golden age. Postmillennialists cite the progress seen in the world as inaugurating a conclusion of the millennium.[5]

Sure seems like we've got a long way to go, doesn't it?

They believe the millennium should not be looked upon as a literal thousand years but rather a symbolic period and, in fact, it may last well longer than 1,000 years.

In contrast to both amillennialism and premillennialism which teaches that the second coming of Christ will occur because the world is becoming more and *more* sinful, postmillennialists view the world as becoming more Christian and *less* sinful. Postmillennialists cite passages such as Daniel 2:44-45, Matthew 13:13-32, 24-14 and Colossians 1:23 as Scriptures that suggest the world will progress before Christ's return.

As for the resurrection of the dead, postmillennialists believe, like the amillennialists, that there will be a general resurrection of both believers and unbelievers that will take place in conjunction with the return of Jesus.

Like the amillennialists, postmillennialists believe there will be a general judgment. There will be a judgment according to the deeds done in the body and people will be judged according to the light they have received (Luke 12:47-48). Those who heard the gospel will be judged according to their attitude toward Christ.[6]

Some postmillennialists view the tribulation as a brief time of persecution that will occur immediately before the millennium. Others known as *"Preterists,"* believe that the great tribulation describes the seven years of the first Jewish-Roman War which culminated in 70 AD with the destruction of the Temple at Jerusalem.

> *"Lift up your head, redemption draweth nigh!"*
> *Gordon Jensen*

The famous preacher, Jonathan Edwards, as well as such theologians as B. B. Warfield, Augustus H. Strong and Reformed theologian R. C. Sproul are noted as prominent believers in postmillennialism.[7]

Signs of the Times

Many today believe that the signs of the times are all around us. Twenty years ago, we sang this song:

> *"Years of time have come and gone*
> *Since I first heard it told*
> *How my Jesus is coming back again*
> *And if back then, it seems so real,*
> *Then I just can't help but feel*
> *How much closer His coming is today*
> *Signs of the times are everywhere*
> *And there's a brand new feeling in the air*
> *So keep your eyes upon the Eastern sky*
> *Lift up your head, redemption draweth nigh.*
> *Wars and strife on every hand*
> *And violence fills our land*
> *Still some people doubt He'll ever come again*

But the Word is true my friend
He'll redeem those born again
Don't lose hope, my friend, Christ Jesus will descend."[13]

Wars and strife? Violence fills the land? Jesus promised His disciples that He would return. There would be signs before His coming. Many will claim to be Messiah and people will be deceived by these false messiahs. There'll be an uprise in wars, famine, earthquakes and disease. Believers in Christ will be persecuted and killed, but will witness far and wide, even to important world leaders. Some will be betrayed by family and friends and some will turn away from the faith. There'll be a general increase in wickedness and we'll all see fearful signs straight from the pits of Hell.

The Antichrist

Jerusalem will be surrounded by armies. The "abomination of desolation" will occur. The Bible explains, *"So when you see standing in the holy place 'the abomination that causes desolation,' spoken of through the prophet Daniel, let the reader understand (Matthew 24:15)."*

This is referring to Daniel 9:27, which says, *"He will confirm a covenant with many for one 'seven.' In the middle of the 'seven' he will put an end to sacrifice and offering. And on a wing of the temple he will set up an abomination that causes desolation, until the end that is decreed is poured out on him."*

In 167 B.C. a Greek ruler by the name of Antiochus Epiphanies set up an altar to Zeus over the altar of burnt offerings in the Jewish temple in Jerusalem. He also sacrificed a pig on the altar in the Temple in Jerusalem. This event is known as the "abomination of desolation."

In Matthew 24:15, Jesus was referring to the Antichrist who will do something very similar to what Antiochus Epiphanies did. It is the Antichrist who, in the end times, will establish a "covenant" with Israel for seven years and then break it by doing something similar to the abomination of desolation in the Jewish temple in Jerusalem.

Whatever the future abomination of desolation is, it'll surely leave no doubt in anyone's mind that the one perpetrating it is the person known as the Antichrist. Revelation 13:14 describes him making some kind of image which all are forced to worship. Turning the temple of the Living God into a place of worship for the Antichrist is truly an "abomination."

Many feel that way about the Dome Of The Rock, the Muslim shrine which stands directly over the visual center of a platform known, even today, as the Temple Mount and the site of the former Jewish and Solomon's Temple. This Second Jewish Temple was destroyed during the Roman siege of Jerusalem in 70 AD. Inside the Dome is supposedly the very rock where Abraham is said to have almost sacrificed his son, Isaac, in obedience to God. The Muslims claim it's not Abraham's rock, but rather the place where Muhammad ascended into Heaven after his Night Journey to Jerusalem (Qur'an 17). It dates back to 688 AD.

Israel actually took control of the Dome of the Rock during its victory in the Six-Day War in 1967. But, a few hours after the Israeli flag was hoisted, General Moshe Dayan ordered it lowered in order to "keep the peace," and gave the place to the Muslims.

Anyway, those who are alive and remain during the tribulation should be watchful for that this abomination of desolation event, for it will signal the beginning of the worst of the tribulation period. More important, it will signal that the return of the Lord Jesus is imminent.

Is the Antichrist living today? You decide. Jesus tells us, *"Be always on the watch, and pray that you may be able to escape all that is about to happen, and that you may be able to stand before the Son of Man"* (Luke 21:36).

There'll be a tribulation like never before. Jerusalem will be trampled upon, false prophets will be performing miracles, the sun will darken, the moon will not shine, the stars will fall, there will be severe ocean activity and people will faint in fear. The number of the beast, 666, will be marked in the right hand or forehead of everyone (Revelation 13:16), the number of complete imperfection. Did you know, that even today, the number 666 is "police code" for "country-wide emergency?"

> *Is the Antichrist living today? You decide.*

The Revelation

God's book of end times is Revelation. Most believe that Revelation predicts future events, but some, the Preterists, believe that the Bible's final Book describes events already history. The Book, the "real" title of which is *"The Revelation [of Jesus Christ] to Saint John The Divine* [parentheses mine]*,"* induces four main interpretive approaches:

> The "preterist" sees all or most of the events in Revelation as having already occurred by the end of the 1st century.
>
> The "historicist" sees Revelation as a survey of church history from apostolic times to the present.
>
> The "idealist" sees Revelation as a depiction of the struggle between good and evil, and,
>
> The "futurist" sees Revelation as prophecy of events to come, such as the Gospels' *Judgment of the Nations*, dividing the blessed and cursed.

Of the four, only the futurist approach interprets Revelation in the same grammatical-historical method as the rest of Scripture. It is also a better fit with Revelation's own claim to be prophecy.

The Book of Revelation is highly symbolic. Because of this fact, many false religionists have attempted to exploit the message of the narrative to their own theological ends. The Apocalypse has become a happy hunting ground for some religious cultists who seek biblical support for their peculiar doctrines.

Just check the internet! But, make sure you have your Bible ready!

The 144,000

For instance, twice in Revelation, mention is made of a group consisting of 144,000. The "Jehovah's Witnesses" have almost no clue to the distinction between the literal and the figurative language in the Bible, and so, they literalize the number 144,000 in these two contexts, and ridiculously argue that only 144,000 people will gain heaven.

Walk to the Future

With the exception of the futurist approach, all of the other approaches interpret the Scriptures as saying 144,000 is symbolically the totality, that is, the complete number of the church, "12,000 taken from every tribe of the sons of Israel." 12,000 times 12 = 144,000.

Much of the confusion regarding the 144,000 is a result of the false doctrine of the Jehovah's Witnesses, who claim that 144,000 is a limit to the number of people who will reign with Christ in Heaven and spend eternity with God.

Those 144,000 have what the Jehovah's Witnesses call the heavenly hope.

Those who are *not* among the 144,000 will enjoy what they call the earthly hope, a paradise on Earth ruled by Christ *and* the 144,000.

Clearly, one can see that Jehovah's Witness teaching sets up a caste society in the afterlife with a ruling class (of the 144,000) and those who are ruled.

> *By the way, the 144,000 have already been chosen, and you're not one of them! Sorry!*

By the way, the 144,000 have already been chosen, and you're not one of them!

Sorry!

Of course, the Bible teaches no such "dual class" doctrine.

Some believe that a literal battle will occur in a valley near Megiddo near the end of time ("*har*" meaning valley, Megiddo, the "mountain," thus har-megiddo, or Armageddon), yet others view Armageddon as only a symbol of an ultimate conflict between good and evil.

The truth is, praise the Lord, Jesus will appear in the sky, the trumpet will sound and angels will minister to gather God's elect (Matthew 24-25, Mark 13 and Luke 21). And when Jesus comes, the Antichrist will be overthrown and destroyed (I Thessalonians 4:17 and II Thessalonians 2). So there!

Through all these interpretations, remember this: God is Love.

So, Then, What Should We Believe?

Like the amillennialists, I, too, am delightfully happy in my new life as a Christ follower. Since I was born-again, my new life here on Earth is wonderful and to me, Heaven is but the graduation from a course I have fully enjoyed.

Still, one can't help but thrill at the picture of Heaven with its streets of gold and walls of jasper. How we Christians cry for those unbelievers who'll be able to see Heaven through the clear walls of jasper but not be able to get there!

"End times" will mean being in the presence of our Savior and our loved ones, and an eternal life of enjoyment. Most important, we will be judged by our Lord as pure, as pure as Adam was in the First Creation. God will look upon us and say that it is "very good."

It will be very good to Walk With God.

I'm a premillennial dispensational pretribulationist, though I don't often call myself that because I rarely get all that out of my mouth at the same time! And, don't ask me to write it without a spell-checker!

I'm a premillennialist because I believe that a Christian millennium without Christ is not a kingdom. In all due respect for my friends who might debate that, how can anyone see the present world as the definition of a Christian kingdom? To the contrary, from 2000-2005, Islam grew faster than any other world religion at 1.84%, which is a pretty big gain when one considers the number of their members.[12] To the postmillennialists, I can offer some hope in that Christianity increased 1.32%, but that's still a far cry from "evangelizing the world." I believe Christ will come, and when He does, He will establish his kingdom at the beginning of his thousand-year reign.

I am a dispensationalist in my beliefs that only a literal interpretation of the Scriptures is reliable and it's hard to move from that position. Besides, dividing up man's history into seven parts makes it more easy to understand. It makes sense to me.

I am a pretribulationist because it's hard to envision Christ leaving Christians here to suffer through a tribulation, beyond that which people may say we are undergoing now, and surely not a violent kind of which some speak. Besides, it's fun to tell my friends that I'll see them, *"here, there or in the air (during the Rapture)!"*

A summary position on end times? It must be the same as our Brother Paul, when he said, *"For me to live is Christ, to die is gain"* (Philippians 1:21).

Brother Peter said, *"The Word of the Lord endures forever"* (I Peter 1:25). Based on that, we can make the following 10 predictions for the coming year:

1. The Bible will still have all the answers.
2. Prayer will still be the most powerful thing on Earth.
3. The Holy Spirit will still move.
4. God will still honor the praises of His people.
5. There will still be God-anointed preaching.
6. There will still be singing of praise to God.
7. God will still pour out blessings upon His people.
8. Jesus will still love you.
9. There will still be room at the Cross.
10. Jesus will still save the lost when they come to Him.

Did you ever notice that a car's windshield is so large and the rear view mirror is so small? That's a good picture, because our past is not as important as our future. And, whatever our thinking about end times, the Truth is we should look ahead and move on.

Until He calls, let us work...

...but even so, come Lord Jesus (Revelation 22:20).

---

[1] Enns, Paul, *The Moody Handbook of Theology* (Chicago, Moody Publishers, 2008), pg. 385.

[2] Talbot, Louis, T., *God's Plan of the Ages* (Grand Rapids Eerdmans, 1936), pg. 196.

[3] Apostasy is the total rejection of Christianity by a baptized person who, having at one time professed the Christian faith, publicly rejects it. It is distinguished from heresy, which is limited to the rejection of one or more Christian doctrines by one who maintains an overall adherence to Jesus Christ.

[4] Berkhof, Louis, *Systematic Theology* (Grand Rapids: Eerdmans, 1941), pg. 722.

[5] Boettner, Loraine, *The Millennium* (Nutley, NJ: Presbyterian and Reformed, 1957), pg. 14.

[6] Hodge, Charles, *Systematic Theology*, 3 viols. (Reprint. London, Clarke, 1960), 3:838-844.

[7] Sproul, R. C., *What Is Reformed Theology* (Grand Rapids: Baker Books, 1997).

[8] Pentecost, J. Dwight, *Things to Come* (Grand Rapids: Zondervan, 1959), pg. 158.

[9] Ladd, George E., "Historic Premillennialism," in *The Meaning of the Millennium* (IL: InterVarsity Press, 2001), pp. 29-32.

[10] Ibid, pg. 39.

[11] Ibid.

[12] *The List: The World's Fastest-Growing Religions* (Carnegie Endowment for International Peace), May 2007.

[13] *"Redemption Draweth Nigh,"* by Gordon Jensen (Nashville, TN.: John T. Benson, 1975.

Epilogue

So, there are 12 Ways To Walk With God:
1. In reading the Word.
2. Understanding our limitations and our possibilities as creatures made in God's own image.
3. Saved to the uttermost.
4. Blood bought and sin-free.
5. Directed every moment by a loving Lord Jesus.
6. Guided by the Holy Spirit.
7. Hovered over by a loving God.
8. In worship of all Three Persons: God, Jesus and the Holy Spirit.
9. In concert with angels sent to minister to us, and in defiance of devils over whom we are more than conquerors.
10. Surrounded by the Church and its fellow Christians.
11. Created to be victors over every offense of the devil and life on Earth.
12. Comforted in knowing our future.

I really hope you enjoyed this book. I hope you learned something, even one thing, that'll really help you. I hope you realize what I realized before writing it, that God rewards us with blessings proportional to our ability to receive them.

If a Christian knows how he or she is saved, how marvelous a gift it is for which our Friend Jesus gave His life, and what a wonderful Plan God had to present that gift to us, then we can be more sure in our salvation, more certain of our place in the Lamb's Book of Life, more sure of our destiny in Heaven.

If we're confident that, as a born-again believer, we're never alone, what a good thing that is! If we're fortified every moment by the Holy Spirit of God that indwells us and connects with the our spirit that God gave us at our creation, if we're comforted in knowing there are angels who come to surround and camp around us to protect us, to bring to us God's message of love, wow, that's got to encourage us.

Even the sincere knowledge that we're not haphazardly made, but created in the image and likeness of the Triune God, gives us a lighthearted step as we Walk With God.

My prayer is that you're truly saved to the uttermost, blood bought and sin-free by the unmerited forgiveness and undeserved favor of God. I pray that you're hovered over by Him, guided by the Holy Spirit and our Lord, Jesus. I pray that you're convinced that you're designed for victory, victory, victory over each and every assault that the devil and this ol' world might throw at you.

Oh, Satan will seek, but he can never devour the child of God.

If somehow, by, through or between the pages of this book, God brought His loving message to you in that kind of way, then this book was worth reading, and writing!

And, that's my fervent desire.

Blessed Friend, may you Walk With God from this point on, equipped and encouraged as His Child. May you touch others with His love. May you be a help to every person He sends your way. May you find it a joy to love the Lord your God with all your heart, all your soul, all your mind and all your strength, until Jesus comes again.

Oh, Victory in Jesus, my Savior Forever,
He sought me and he bought me with his redeeming blood.
He loved me ere I knew him, and all my love is due him,
He plunged me to victory Beneath the Cleansing Flood!
   And then I cried "Dear Jesus, Come and heal my broken spirit"
And somehow Jesus came and brought to me the victory.

We are victors. Hallelujah! We are Precious in the Eyes of Jesus! Walk With God in a joyful way today!

God bless you, special one!

You are loved,
Buddy
Dr. M. S. Buddy Merrick

Bible Translations

The Bible was originally written using 11,280 Hebrew, Aramaic and Greek words, but the typical English translation uses only around half that amount of words. Because the meanings of words in the original languages can't always be duplicated in English, this book uses several translations, depending on which seems to be the clearest for that application. Below are some of the more popular English translations that are available today:

Amplified Bible, Grand Rapids: Zondervan (1965), abbreviated AMP

Contemporary English Version, New York: American Bible Society (1995), abbreviated CEV

God's Word Translation, Grand Rapids: World Publishing, Inc. (1995), abbreviated GWT

Holman Christian Standard Bible, Nashville, TN: Holman Bible Publishers, abbreviated HCSB

King James Version, Public Domain. Originally published in 1611 as authorized by King James I of England.

Living Bible, Wheaton, IL: Tyndale House Publishers (1979), abbreviated LB *New American Bible,* Colorado Springs: Navpress (1993), abbreviated NAB

New American Standard Bible, Anaheim, CA: Foundation Press (1973), abbreviated NASB

New International Version, Colorado Springs: International Bible Society, abbreviated NIV

New Living Translation, Wheaton, IL: Tyndale House Publishers, abbreviated NLT

New Revised Standard Version, Grand Rapids: Zondervan (1990), abbreviated NRSV

Today's English Version / Good News Translation, New York: American Bible Society (1992), abbreviated TEV or GNT

How To Be Born-Again

What does it mean to be "born again?" Answer: To be re-generated, re-created into a new being, by the power of the Holy Spirit, by God Himself. Everything changes in one's inner self.

The Bible tells us that Jesus Himself used the phrase in a conversation with a man named Nicodemus. He had approached Jesus at night. He was curious about Jesus and the "kingdom" of God.

Jesus told him, *"Unless you are born again, you cannot see the Kingdom of God."*

Nicodemus replied, *"How can a man be born when he is old?"*

Nicodemus was a good guy. He obeyed God's law. He was a respected leader of the Jewish community. Yet, something was lacking. He was religious. Many people today are religious. They may say, *"I go to church"* or *"I pray regularly."* But they aren't born of the Spirit that is God. They're not "connected" to God.

Becoming born again, experiencing a new birth, starts when the Holy Spirit (God) convicts a person that he or she is a sinner. Because of sin, that person is spiritually dead. With natural, or unspiritual eyes, he or she can never understand the things of God because the things of God are spiritual things. But God loves us so much, He, the Holy Spirit, will "connect" one-on-one with our spirit if we will only ask.

To be born again, then, simply requires that a sinner (we are all sinners says Romans 3:23) admits the sin, repents of it, accepts that Jesus is the Son of God, and commits to Jesus as Lord from that point on. Jesus told Nicodemus, *"God so loved the world, that He gave His only begotten Son, that whosoever believes in Him will never perish, but have eternal life."*

To be almost saved is to be totally lost, so why not settle it right now? Confess your sins. Ask Jesus to save you. *"Everyone who calls on the name of the Lord will be saved"* (Acts 2:21).

Once you have received Jesus into your life, tell someone. Find a Bible-preaching church and ask to be baptized as a public expression of your new faith (Romans 6:4; Colossians 2:6).

Write to me, Dr. Buddy Merrick, 141 Highland Terrace Circle, Denison, Texas 75020, and let me know about your decision. I promise I'll pray for you, I'll send you Billy Graham's booklet, *"Steps To Peace With God,"* and I'll rejoice with you in your new life.

God bless you, precious friend. You are loved!

About the Author

Dr. Buddy Merrick received his Doctor of Divinity Degree from Master's International School of Divinity as the Honor Graduate of the Class of 2009. He also earned a Liberal Arts Degree from Union College and, after study at New York University's School of Commerce, he graduated with a perfect 4.0 cume from Wayland Baptist University with a Bachelor of Science degree in Occupational Education, and a double major in Religion and Business Administration. He also studied at Southern Seminary in Louisville, Rutgers University and Northeastern University, and later taught as a guest lecturer at Hawaii Pacific University and elsewhere.

Lieutenant Colonel Merrick is a former helicopter pilot who served in the Viet Nam and Persian Gulf eras, and commanded Navy helicopters with HS-9 from the U.S.S. Essex during the Cuban Quarantine. Later, he authored the majority of the *"History of Armed Forces Radio and Television,"* published by the U. S. Department of Defense, while working in Washington, DC. He is a graduate of the U. S. Naval Aviation Program, the U. S. Army Armor Officers Advanced Course and Phase One of the U. S. Army Command and General Staff College. He taught military tactics to company commanders who served in Operation Desert Storm, and led services, choirs and Bible studies aboard ship, on the base and in the field. He retired after 35 years of service in the U. S. Navy, Army, Army

National Guard and Army Reserve with more than fifteen medals and honors.

Rev. Merrick is a national gospel recording artist, an evangelist, an ordained minister in the Southern Baptist Convention and a former co-owner of Christian television station WJAL-TV in the Washington, DC, market area. His gospel group, *Buddy Merrick & Praise,* recorded hits with Nashville's Homeland Records and Morning Star Records, including many songs he wrote which are still played today across the country. He has preached and sung all over America for more than 50 years.

Today, Dr. Merrick teaches a weekly Bible Seminar at Parkside Baptist Church in Denison, Texas, and of course, still sings and preaches. He no longer runs the marathons, though.

Dr. Merrick loves classic cars and hot rods. He built several national champion cars including a custom 1987 Corvette, a 1932 Ford roadster and a pearl-white1966 Cadillac convertible. He played high school football, coached men's baseball and basketball teams and loves the Dallas Mavericks and the Cowboys.

Buddy lives in Denison, Texas, with his wife Carol, with whom he has raised five children of their own and three more adopted boys. To his great delight, all of them are also born-again Christians as well.

Buddy Merrick loves the Lord and serves God with all his heart.

Outstanding Graduate Award

The Outstanding Graduate Award is presented to the graduate who has given himself or herself in the area of ministry to which God has called His servant. In addition, the award recipient will have proven performances in other vital areas of life, such as the church, family, secular work, and service to one's country.

The recipient, who has proven himself worthy of this award tonight, has served faithfully as a minister, husband, father, successful businessman, and defender of his country. In all these, he has distinguished himself while honoring God in all things.

He is known as a singer, a recording artist, and retired as a Lieutenant Colonel after a military career of 35 years, serving as a Navy Seaman, as well as an aviator with both the US Army and US Navy. He received the Meritorious Service Medal with Oak Leaf Cluster, the National Defense Medal with Bronze Star, and a Presidential Unit Citation among other awards.

Now, after more hard work and dedication to his Lord and the people he has been called to serve, he comes this weekend to receive the Doctor of Divinity Degree.

> NO SOLDIER IN ACTIVE SERVICE ENTANGLES HIMSELF IN THE AFFAIRS OF EVERYDAY LIFE, SO THAT HE MAY PLEASE THE ONE WHO ENLISTED HIM AS A SOLDIER.
> 2 TIMOTHY 2:4

The recipient of the 2009 Outstanding Graduate Award is

MEREDITH SAMUEL "BUDDY" MERRICK
Presented on August 1, 2009
By Dr. Gary K. Fair, D. P. Th., Vice President
Masters International School of Divinity
Evansville, Indiana

- Death
- Heaven
- Hell
- Rapture
- Tribration
- Last Judgement
- Second Coming
- Anti christ
- Victory + mill
- Messi Age
- Disp
- Pell